BILL TALBERT'S WEEKEND TENNIS

BILL TALBERT'S WEEKEND TENNIS

How to Have Fun and Win at the Same Time

by BILL TALBERT

with Gordon Greer

Illustrations by Frank Modell

Doubleday & Company, Inc., Garden City, New York

My thanks to *World Tennis* and *Sports Illustrated* for the help they have given me and to all those fanatic weekend tennis players who contributed ideas and suggestions.

Library of Congress Catalog Card Number 77–103779
Copyright © 1970 by William F. Talbert and Gordon Greer
All Rights Reserved
Printed in the United States of America

For Nancy, Pike, and Peter

CONTENTS

BILL TALBERT'S WEEKEND TENNIS

WHAT'S SO GREAT ABOUT TENNIS

HEAVEN ONLY knows how many tennis balls I've hit in the years I've been playing this crazy game. Millions? Tens of millions? Billions perhaps? How many dollars is our national debt now? Maybe that's the number I'm looking for. People sometimes wonder if I don't find it boring, just knocking a little ball back and forth across a net after doing it for roughly forty years. No, sir, I do not. When I was a kid growing up in Cincinnati, I used to play tennis six hours every day—eight or ten whenever I could swing it. Now that I'm fifty, the sessions are shorter, but I still enjoy playing every day. For my money, tennis is the optimum sport. I'm totally in love with the game.

There are other games I'm fond of—golf, for example—but they aren't in the same class with tennis. Actually, I'm reluctant to call golf a sport at all. It's approximately as strenuous as walking your dog—less so, if you use those little gocarts. Golf could be described as the ideal activity for people who hate to exercise. Its usefulness in keeping you physically trim is about on a par with poker. Take a look at those golfers in the televised tournaments. Nicklaus. Boros. Bob Murphy. Miller Barber. Have you noticed the size of the stomachs on those guys? When a foursome like that comes clomping onto the green, you half expect the whole thing to sink. Tennis players, on the other hand, are all slim, strong, and handsome. Or slim, lithe, and pretty, if they're female.

I also like team sports—my early childhood was mostly baseball—but it bugs me when school kids have it drummed into their heads that only team sports, especially football, build character. Their advertised advantage over individual sports is that they teach the necessity of working well with others and of subordinating private interests to the group's. Possibly they do, but such lessons have their limits. Sometimes self-reliance is a more valuable virtue, and that's what you develop playing tennis. You're out there all alone, or with only one partner, and you lack the opportunity provided by football for letting ten other players do the work (or take the blame). From tennis, you learn to accept responsibility. A direct confrontation with the guy across the net, one against one, in full view of the public, builds just as much character as "getting along with others," which smacks a wee bit of conformity—or at least so it seems to a tennis player's mind, most tennis players being stanch individualists.

Besides, what kind of future does a team sport provide? Pretend you're a college football hero with all the pretty coeds swooning at your feet. Fine, but what comes after that? Perhaps, if you're good enough, a professional contract and the chance to have your limbs cracked on Sunday afternoons for a half dozen autumns or so. And what happens after you quit? Do you round up twenty-one friends and rent a pasture when you feel in the mood for some exercise? The alternatives are to sit around the house and grow fat or to take up a sport you can play your whole lifetime—in other words, switch to tennis.

I'm happy to report that many athletes do the latter. They hang up their shoulder pads or spikes or whatever, look around for something to fill the sudden void with, and belatedly discover tennis. Just from my personal circle of friends, I could give you a dozen examples. Otto Graham. John Brodie. Bobby Brown. Crazy Legs Hirsch. Ralph Kiner. Hank Greenberg. Each of them learned tennis only after his retirement, and each now says he should have started sooner. Greenberg plays at every opportunity he gets these days, occasionally as my doubles partner. I must say, he isn't too bad, old Henry. But remember how he used to hit a baseball so hard? Well, oddly enough, he plays tennis just the opposite way; he's what we sometimes refer to as a "pusher." He realizes that his game would be considerably better—and he'd enjoy it even more because of course he'd *win* more often—if he'd begun at an earlier age. Fortunately, he still has lots of time to improve in. King Gustaf V of Sweden played far into his eighties, and Charlie Chaplin, the last time I met him on the court, was seventy-five and by no means a pushover. They tell me his game remains steady past eighty. Oona, his wife, still can't beat him.

Frankly, I enjoy a game where men compete with women. The segregation of the sexes in so many other sports drastically reduces their appeal. Maybe that's the reason why I've never felt envious of Bart Starr or Gordie Howe or Harmon Killebrew. They're all superior athletes, of course—the best, or close to it, in their respective fields of sport—but do they play against the likes of Jinx Falkenburg and Ava Gardner? Tennis players do. At least *I* did. How often does Bill Russell take the court, would you estimate, against Jacqueline Kennedy Onassis? I've done so on several occasions. Her game, in case you're curious, might best be called "determined." She never concedes a point. Bob Kennedy, her late brother-in-law, had the same characteristic. He was an extremely energetic competitor. Yet you couldn't really say that he was a particularly good player, because he hadn't taken time to learn the basics. Once I played Jackie in a mixed doubles match—her partner was Dick Savitt and mine was Gloria Schiff—and caught her out of position with a drop shot. She tried so hard to reach it that she fell on her face. In the process, she not only broke her racket in half but also split the seam of her slacks. What *Women's Wear Daily* wouldn't have given for *that* picture!

Lawn tennis has always had a semisocial status, and you can meet a lot of fascinating people on the court, people from almost every walk of life. (It is *not* just a pasttime for affluent snobs.) The majority of the household names I've made friends with— plus hundreds of fine people whose lives are less publicized—I never would have met in a million years except as a tennis player. If I mention a few of them once in a while, I hope you won't accuse me of name-dropping. It's simply that I've played a lot of tennis with celebrities, and the strengths and weaknesses they reveal on the court are as instructive as anyone else's. A certain small percentage of them are fairly good players—Charlton Heston, Ginger Rogers, and General Maxwell D. Taylor are the names that most quickly come to mind in this respect— and others are completely inept. I suppose that of the "famous name" people I've played, the worst was Gary Cooper, the late film star. He was a wonderful guy and he loved to play tennis and, ironically, no actor looked more like an athlete than the one who portrayed Lou Gehrig in the movies. Cooper walked like an athlete, he dressed like an athlete—I never saw a man who looked better in tennis flannels—but he had no co-ordination whatsoever. I mean none. Even Peter Ustinov could have blown him off the court, and Peter isn't exactly Rod Laver. The most interesting aspect of Ustinov's game is the bizarre way he has of serving. Somehow, Peter twists himself the whole way around so that he's facing directly away from the net, as if furtively looking for a friend in the grandstand, at the moment he delivers the ball. Damnedest thing you ever laid eyes on. My two sons were with me the first time I played him, and they laughed so hard they fell off their chairs.

Both of my boys, Pike and Peter, play tennis, and sometimes so does Nancy, my wife. Often we play together. As a husband-and-wife doubles team, as a matter of fact, Nancy and I are still undefeated. That's another of the virtues tennis has in my eyes: you can get the whole family into the act. Maybe my attitude is absurdly archaic, but I like to have my family around me. I'm away from them long enough during work hours. Men who take up bowling or golf or whatever to get out of the house and away from wife and children . . . well, their home lives must be less pleasant than my own. When I was on the tennis tour and the boys were still kids, neither of them old enough to go along with me, I missed them before I was out the front door. I hadn't even gone yet and I was ready to come back. Finally, when the older boy, Pike, was nine, I took him on a trip around the world with me, and that's the tour I remember most enjoyably.

Athletes are constantly traveling, of course, but these days so is everyone else—and not just to places like Omaha and Boston, but to Lisbon and Calcutta and Capetown. Try to find a baseball fan in one of those cities. Or someone to talk football or basketball with. Chances are, you'll look a long time. Frank Robinson may be a hero in Baltimore, Maryland, but very few people in Bangkok ever heard of him. Tennis, though, is a truly international sport. It's played in every country in the world. I'm well into my second million miles of traveling now, and I've yet to find a single exception. Wherever there's a semblance of civilized life, you can always find someone to play tennis with. And you don't have to buy a lot of costly equipment. Just a racket and some balls are all you need. General Taylor, in a commencement speech he made once at West Point, advised the cadets that in their travels around the world the two things they should always be sure to carry with them were their officer's manual and a tennis racket.

But you can also play tennis without going far from home. It isn't like golf in that respect. There are facilities for tennis in every American city, and I mean *in* the city, not twenty miles distant. Where I live, in Manhattan, near the center of the island, I'm just ten or fifteen minutes from a half dozen places where New Yorkers can go to play tennis—some of them private courts, some public. The golfers among my neighbors leave home in the morning and frequently don't get back before dusk, having spent more time in transit than golfing. That wouldn't be so bad if they got a workout when they played, but all they do is stroll casually through the meadows and woods and study every shot for ten minutes. No kidding, I sometimes have my doubts about golfers. I mean, the ball they're trying to hit is standing *still*, for heaven's sake. How could they possibly miss? What if it were moving about a hundred miles an hour or so, the way a tennis ball frequently is? I suppose what they'd do is let it hit them in the stomach. And probably never feel it.

Personally, I like sports in which you get a little exercise, and the exercise demanded by a single hour of tennis—which means maybe an hour and a half away from the house—is worth four or five days trudging slowly over the countryside, infrequently—or, in my case, frequently swinging a stick.

I also prefer sports in which the players match wits in a one-against-one confrontation. I like to see the winner of a contest determined by the interplay of their individual skills. So many games are just a disguised form of solitaire. You can bowl by yourself, play golf by yourself—your opponents just come along to keep you company. Arnold Palmer always talks about "attacking the course." His attitude is very revealing. It suggests that the primary challenge in golf is provided by the landscape or by par. The opposition, in other words, is inhuman. Palmer could just as easily be out there all alone. Whether the other guys in the tournament are playing well or playing badly affects Arnie's game only indirectly, if at all.

No such statement could be made about tennis. One player plays the way the other player lets him. If anything, tennis seems sometimes *too* personal. Victory is accompanied by a keen sense of conquest, and the loser is sometimes exposed just as thoroughly as if he were lying on a psychiatrist's couch. If you ever want instant insight into a person's true character, get him in a session on the tennis court.

There are three kinds of demands made on those who play tennis—physical, psychological, and mental. No other sport I've ever engaged in blends them in such a rich combination. And you have to excel in all three areas if you hope to win consistently at tennis. Played properly, it's a difficult game. Physically, you need speed, strength, agility, quick reflexes, steadiness, and stamina. Psychologically, you must be able to stay cool and unflappable while trying simultaneously to bug your opponent in a never-ending contest of wills. And mentally, what you're faced with is a rapid-fire chess game combined with a geometry lesson. No wonder it's been labeled the thinking man's sport, the complete sport, the ultimate sport.

There are only two things I dislike about tennis. The first of these is losing. I'd never lose a point if I could help it. A friend of mine, a medical man, Dr. Irving S. Cooper, who devised the freeze treatment for Parkinson's disease, has exactly the opposite feeling. He can't stand to *win* a tennis match. I suspect that if he were ahead of you five games to love, and leading in the sixth game 40–0 on his serve, he'd ease up and ultimately lose. I ascribe this tendency to the sense of compassion that all good doctors possess. He knows how losers suffer in tennis, and as a doctor he has seen enough suffering. I'd probably make a terrible doctor.

Other players sometimes claim they're just having fun, that they really don't care who wins. Frankly, I think these people are just kidding themselves. Winning, in sports as in anything else, is a lot more fun than losing. The way to have fun is to win gracefully.

But winning isn't the *only* thing that matters in tennis, and I don't mean to suggest that it is. I said there were two things I dislike about the game, the first of which is losing. The second is winning when no one has fun. I'm bothered by the growing popularity among weekenders of the so-called "big" style of play—the monstrous serve followed by the rush to the net, then the hard volley that ends the point quickly. This bang-bang approach is inevitable, I suppose, in an era when most other popular sports have put a premium on their more ex-plosive aspects. In baseball, all the batters seem to swing for home runs now. In football, the "long bomb" is in vogue. "That's where the money is," we're constantly informed, or, "It makes it a more exciting game to watch." But more en-joyable to play? I think not. What fun is playing tennis, even *winning* at tennis, if your whole game is a blistering serve? You ace your opponent, he retrieves the ball, and you do it all over again. That isn't tennis, that's swat-and-go-fetch-it—the same tiresome game little ten-year-old boys play before they've dis-covered the fine points of tennis or learned to sustain a rally.

Don't get me wrong. I'm in favor of the "big" game for serious players of exceptional ability competing at the top or aspiring to. You *must* have the "big" game to survive against a player like Arthur Ashe, say, or Rod Laver. I was up there at the top once myself, and I know. But weekenders and club players who ape the stars' tactics—without, in most cases, the skill to bring them off—are draining all the pleasure from the sport.

This book is intended for amateurs and duffers, for weekend players real or potential who would like some nontechnical ad-vice. I'm assuming you fit that category. My guess is that you don't play too often—or too well—but you enjoy tennis and you want to improve. By getting better mileage from your limited talents, you'd like to have more fun and win more matches. Good. I think the two of us will get along just fine.

Chapter 2

THE THINGS WEEKEND PLAYERS DO WRONG

On Sunday afternoons when I'm home in New York, I like to wander over to the courts in Central Park and watch the weekend tennis players do their thing. On a typical weekend afternoon, you'll see grandmothers, children, husband-and-wife doubles teams, secretaries, doctors, construction workers, hippies—all of them shattering the ancient misconception that tennis is primarily a genteel lawn game preserved in ritzy country clubs and monopolized by the idle rich. It beats me how this image has persisted so long. Actually, if you jotted down the names of the top players—either past or present, it makes little difference—your list would be dominated by guys who got their start on public courts. Ashe, Gonzales, Kramer, Budge, Seixas, Trabert, Riggs, Mulloy—not a single rich playboy in the crowd. Far from being members of any wealthy elite during our years on the tennis circuit, we were always wondering where our next dollar might come from.

So I feel a special affinity for public court players, but I concede that to watch them play is often frustrating. It bothers me that they keep making the same old mistakes, over and over again. Mind you, I'm not talking about unavoidable flaws, imperfections that might plague even world-class players. I mean *basic* errors, silly errors, inexcusable errors really, that show they just aren't thinking. Sometimes the weekenders I watch in Central Park ask me after the match to give them pointers. I'll bet if

I've told one of them, I must have told a thousand: "You aren't getting your racket back soon enough." Here comes the ball at him, already over the net now, and he hasn't even begun to get ready. When he *finally* cocks his arm back, the ball is nearly past him and the racket seems to be politely opening a door for it. "You can't make a return on your backswing," I tell him. "The instant you see where a tennis ball is headed, get your racket in position to hit it."

Many basic errors are so common among weekend players that I'll bet I could enumerate a dozen you're guilty of, even without seeing you lift a racket. Think not? Well, maybe you're much better than the average. But just for fun, why don't we try it? We'll make a mental tour around the courts in Central Park—I think there are thirty of them, something like that—and list the basic errors we see committed. Then check whatever number of these mistakes you make yourself, and see if the total isn't twelve or more.

COURT 1. Variety, they say, is the spice of life. It's also an essential of good tennis. A predictable pattern like this lady here is using is a serious handicap. Her first serve is invariably a slice to the forehand. Her second is always a soft spin aimed to the backhand. See? It never fails. After three cross-court drives, she hits the fourth shot down the line. She follows every lob with a drop shot. Her strokes are as regular and as lacking in surprise as the chimes that toll the hour on Big Ben. Once you know the pattern—and it doesn't take long—you can beat a player like this with no trouble.

COURT 2. I congratulate this fellow for bringing the lob into play—a shot much neglected by most weekend players—but he gives it the same altitude no matter how he uses it: defensively, to recover from a vulnerable position, or offensively, when his opponent comes too close to the net. His failure to differentiate between the two uses deprives the lob of much of its effectiveness. If it helps, you can think of them as completely different shots. A defensive lob should be high—maybe twenty or thirty feet. An offensive lob should stay down around ten and be used only when your opponent's nose is hanging over the net— or occasionally to his backhand side. How many good backhand overheads have you seen?

COURT 3. If you watch that girl serve, you'll see she chases every toss. One time she'll throw it straight over her head. The next time, while attempting the same kind of serve, it's in back of her or off to one side. No wonder she sprays her serves. Her mistake is in starting the toss much too low, with her arm straight down by her side. Then she jerks it up quickly, acquires too much momentum, and aimlessly launches the ball into flight as if she were trying to put it into orbit. Remember when you're serving not to hurry your toss. Just lift the ball gently as if you were putting it on a shelf only a couple feet higher than your head. And don't start the toss any lower than your waist. A big wind-up just deprives you of control.

COURT 4. The fellow at this end looks like a natural athlete, much the better player of the two. He moves well, hits the ball hard, has good concentration—so how come he's behind in the score? Well, you'll notice he tries to win every point outright. He isn't content to go along with the percentages and let the other guy lose a few. Or maybe he doesn't know about the percentages. Anyhow, he keeps attempting spectacular winners, and in accordance with the odds, he usually misses.

Tennis records show that for every point won, about four other points are lost. Do you clearly understand the distinction? You *win* a point when you follow Willie Keeler's advice and "hit 'em where they ain't." You can do it with either an ace or an unreachable placement; your opponent doesn't touch it, and you win outright. You *lose* a point when you hit it into the net or out-of-bounds. And the latter happens four times more often than the former.

Outright winners are more satisfying, of course, but the statistics show how foolish it is to try this kind of flashy shot too often. If you've maneuvered your opponent into leaving a big opening, then, certainly: try to put the shot away. But other times, just concentrate on getting the ball back with as much pace as your ability permits and your chances of success will be much greater. Your opponent will eventually reward you with an error. Gardnar Mulloy and I pursued this philosophy when we played together as doubles partners. "Above all, get the ball back," was our principal rule. "Make the *other* team take the big risks." We played in a hundred tournaments together and managed to win ninety-four. That's a reliable indication that it works.

COURT 5. Did you happen to hear what that boy told his friend a minute ago? He said he saw Clark Graebner play a match the other day and he hit one serve so hard he broke his racket. So now, of course, the boy wants to serve just like Graebner. Look at him flailing away over there. It'll probably set his game back five years. I'm anxious to have tennis receive greater publicity—I'd like to see more matches on television, for example—but I wish there were a way to keep beginners and weekend players from attempting to copy the stars. The only way you can win is by using your *own* skills, your *own* style, your *own* array of talents. Try to copy Graebner and you're sunk. Maybe an announcement should precede all televised matches pointing out the possible dangers—like those warnings on cigarette packages. "Attempting to emulate the players on this program may be hazardous to your game."

COURT 6. That fellow on the far side strikes me as an actor. At least he has an actor's footwork. By that I mean it's all wrong for tennis. Maybe you've noticed how an actor on the stage always takes his first step with the foot nearest where he's going. If he's planning to walk from left to right, his right foot always makes the first step. That way he keeps facing toward the audience longer. A tennis player should do it just the opposite;

he should always take his first step with his far foot. If you're moving toward your right, you want to pivot on your right foot, but make the first step across with your left. This gives you a better start and swings you into the position from which you should hit the ball: with your hips and shoulders pointed in the direction of flight, just the way a batter stands in baseball.

COURT 7. Look how that woman stoops over for low returns. She ought to be bending her knees. See? There goes another shot into the net. It's hardly any wonder. She can't possibly hold her racket handle parallel to the ground if she doesn't bend her knees to get down to shots like that. She'll either hit the ball straight into the net or shovel it over softly to where her opponent can kill it.

COURT 8. We haven't watched this guy play half a dozen points yet, and already he's blown two easy smashes. There are reasons why a tennis player flubs an easy overhead, but there aren't any excuses for doing it. It simply should never happen. It's like a shortstop misjudging an easy pop fly or a golfer three-putting from two feet. Then why does it happen so often? Sometimes, I believe, because the shot is *too* easy. The player allows it to psych him. ("How embarrassing to *miss* this," starts going through his head.) Or maybe he's too impatient for the ball to come down. He's so anxious for a shot that he can handle for a change that he swings at it prematurely. Or maybe he just takes his eye off the ball. But this guy here has an even worse trait. He's compelled by his sense of showmanship to give a simple shot unnecessary flair. He smashes the ball with every ounce of strength at his command (three-quarter speed would be quite fast enough) and assumes a completely unwarranted risk by trying to hit exactly in the corner. He deserves to miss as many as he does.

COURT 9. That girl has a pretty good serve, all in all. Most of her first serves are landing in, usually deep, carrying fair pace, mostly close to the corner, sometimes to the forehand side, sometimes to the backhand—enough variety so her opponent should be kept guessing. But the truth is, she *isn't* kept guessing. She knows in advance where every serve is coming, and she positions herself to return it. She knows because the server is tipping her off. How? By looking briefly at the spot she's going to hit to. Watch her eyes before she tosses the ball in the air. She telegraphs every one.

Even top players sometimes telegraph their serves—in ways their opponents usually keep to themselves. A few are good enough to get away with it. If your delivery is as powerful as Gonzales', for example, you could probably paint a big white "X" where you're aiming and ace your opponent anyhow. But most players must learn to keep their target a secret—by tossing the ball up the same way each time, by eliminating quirks in their swing or stance, and by not looking directly at the target. (It's a stationary court, it won't move on you.) Even in my heyday as a tennis player, my own serve, sad to say, lacked blistering speed, so I knew I couldn't telegraph my target and still win. I worked very hard at disguising it. Harry Hopman, the long-time captain of the Australian Davis Cup team, used to have his players watch me serve during practice to see if they could find any clues. He offered them a "bob" for every serve they could "read" before my racket strings actually hit the ball. I'm glad to say he didn't lose much money.

COURT 10. Dig old Roger Roundabout here. Wherever he goes, he takes the longest route to get there. His path to the net on that point he just lost reminded me of a zigzag pattern in football, a tight end going out for a pass. Then when his opponent lobbed deep to his forehand, he rushed toward the net post, where the ball passed high above him, stopped, made a 90-degree turn to the right, and hurried back underneath it to the base line. A straight, diagonal path would have saved him five steps and maybe enough time to reach the lob. By the end of the first set, he'll be dragging.

COURT 11. "Keep your eye on the ball, keep your eye on the ball"—I suppose I've said that almost as often as, "You're not getting your racket back soon enough." And now you can understand why. That girl missed the ball by a good six inches because she didn't see how it was curving. She was watching her opponent's advance to the net and planning a passing shot. Tennis balls curve. They carry spin. They take bad bounces. A strong wind blows them all over the place. To hit the ball properly, you *must* keep your eye on it until it touches the strings of your racket. Not until it gets within two or three feet. Until it actually touches the strings.

COURT 12. Here's a guy who seems to know more about compromise than he does about playing tennis. Notice how he returns to the middle of his court after every shot he makes. He probably imagines that's the ideal position because it's equidistant from all four corners. Actually, he couldn't have picked a worse spot. He's lucky his opponent isn't hitting at his feet. He couldn't return one ball out of a hundred that were aimed there. You should never, never, never take a position in the middle—in the so-called no man's land. Stand near the base line or up at the net but (maybe you remember the lyrics of the old ballad) don't mess with Mister In-between.

COURT 13. We've been watching these four gals about fifteen minutes now and they've spent ten of them arguing over the score. In their hour on the court, they'll be lucky to play three games. All you have to do to eliminate these squabbles, so common among weekend players, especially women—though I've played against men who were every bit as bad—is to have the server announce the score before each point. Then you can spend your time playing tennis instead of fighting. The practice is only necessary for a few people, of course. Good players don't need to be reminded of the score; they always have it firmly in mind.

COURT 14. That tall fellow plays doubles as if it were the same game as singles but with twice as many players. It isn't.

The two are fundamentally different. Net play, for example, is more important in doubles; you *must* advance to net if you're to win. Getting the first serve in is more crucial. The tactics differ in significant ways—which this fellow doesn't seem to realize. Notice how every shot he makes is cross-court or down the line. He never hits straight up the middle. That scheme might suffice in a singles match, but in doubles, low down the middle is a good place to hit—frequently the *best* place to hit. For at least a split second, your opponents are uncertain as to which of them ought to return it. They'll sometimes run together, or make the opposite mistake and pull an Alphonse-Gaston act—both stop and watch the ball sail by them untouched, each expecting the other to do the honors.

COURT 15. Look where that lady is standing to serve. Her left foot must be six inches in front of the base line. In a tournament, the umpire would call every serve a fault. But she'd probably get angry if you called it to her attention that she's violating the rules every time. Many weekend players, and club players too, find it convenient to overlook foot faults. Maybe they figure that so many people do it, the law must be intrinsically wrong—something like Prohibition. Anyhow, when you mention it, they often get incensed. Are you accusing them of *cheating*? How dare you, sir! Well, call it what you will, the rule is quite specific: Both feet must remain completely behind the base line or above the court—not on it, until the racket meets the ball. It seems to me a perfectly legitimate rule, and I see no justification for breaking it. Foot faults should not be tolerated on public courts or country club courts any more than they're tolerated at Wimbledon.

COURT 16. Good Lord! Is that guy celebrating Mardi Gras or something? Get a load of that outfit he has on. Green hat, blue socks, a plaid shirt, and checkered tennis shorts—four or five sizes too small. "Hey, buddy! Yeah, you behind the rainbow over there. Can I give you a little advice? If you *must* get your tennis clothes from Ralston Purina, the least you could do is enclose enough boxtops so they'll send you a size that fits!" Traditional white—or now the U. S. Lawn Tennis Association permits pastels—is the rule.

COURT 17. That man made a beautiful shot just then, didn't he? An angled volley from close to the net that drew the other chap way off the court. But then he let the point get away. Did you see how? He returned to a position near the center of the net and his opponent hit behind him for a winner. The mistake is a fairly common one. Many players think they always have to protect their whole court and therefore always stand equidistant between the net posts when actually only part of the court needs protecting. Here, with his opponent far off to the left, this man should have moved that way too. So what if he leaves the right side less guarded? His opponent lacks an angle for hitting there anyway. And by moving just two or three steps left of center he could have reached his opponent's return. Remember that the net is your ally on defense. Usually it shields about a third of your court from possible enemy attack. Your job is not to protect the whole thing—only the remaining two thirds.

COURT 18. Here are two guys who deserve each other. Neither one is using his head. The fellow on this side has his nose over the net, an open invitation to his opponent to lob him— he'd have no chance at all against a good offensive lob—but the other guy never gives it a thought; he hits nothing but forehand drives. The idea in tennis is to use the whole court. If your opponent plays up, hit at his feet, and if he's deep, use short angles—move him about. These chaps are playing as if they were engaged in a game of catch—aiming *at* the other guy instead of *away* from him.

COURT 19. I could shoot people like that dunderhead waving his racket over there, trying to distract the server. That's kid stuff, a bush stunt, bad sportsmanship at its worst. In many ways, tennis is a true test of character. This guy flunks the test.

COURT 20. In some sports, the further ahead you get, the more justified you are in taking chances. In tennis, it doesn't work that way, however. The percentages of the game are unique. Keep in mind that in tennis more points are lost than won—the ratio is roughly four to one—and you lose them by taking risks. A minute ago, this doubles team was comfortably ahead. The pressure was on their opponents. They should have been content to consolidate their lead and force the other side, whose plight was becoming increasingly desperate, to take the chances that so often lead to errors. Instead, they let up and began to play fancy, and now they're behind again. Tennis players who avoid needless risks aren't being chicken; it's just that they appreciate the odds. Don't change a winning game.

COURT 21. That's twice in succession the fellow with the beard there has had his service broken at love—eight straight points he's lost serving. Why in the world does he stick to the same serve? All eight of them were slice serves hit deep to his opponent's forehand. Normally, that's a good place to put a slice serve, but in this instance, it's clearly a mistake. His opponent apparently thrives on them there. All eight of them came back as fast as rockets. Okay, so maybe that's the serve he hits best. Is that a good enough reason not to change? What can he lose by trying something different—a slice to the backhand maybe, or another kind entirely, a cannonball or an American twist? You can't do much worse than drop eight out of eight. A rule of thumb in tennis is that when you're losing, change tactics.

COURT 22. This lad suffers from what I call "baseball player's syndrome." By that I mean he acts as if his position on the court were dictated by stationary bases. If the ball comes wide to his forehand side, he stretches out to reach it, first-baseman fashion, never taking his left foot off the bag. If it comes toward his chest, he swings with a cramped motion, as if standing up to a very tight fast ball. Basically, it's a form of laziness. He considers it too much trouble to move his whole body into the proper hitting position. Naturally, his shots suffer as a consequence. Move your feet—bend your knees.

COURT 23. I'm afraid if we stay at this court much longer we're likely to end up witnesses at a murder trial. WOMAN BLUDGEONS MIXED-DOUBLES PARTNER WITH RACKET will be the headline in the *Daily News*. Personally, I intend to testify on her behalf. Anyone who poaches as excessively as her partner is doing deserves whatever bad end he comes to. He might as well be out there playing singles. And what makes his determination to steal all her shots worse is his remarkable inability to return them. He hits three out of four into the net. Poaching at the invitation of a weaker partner is one thing. Stealing the other person's shots and then blowing them is something else entirely. I hope she lets him have it good and proper.

COURT 24. To execute a successful advance to the net, your approach shot—or follow-in shot, a synonymous term—must be deep enough to allow you sufficient time to get there before your opponent can send the ball back. You saw here what happens if it's shallow. That fellow who started in behind a weak, short backhand got barely as far as no man's land before he was passed by his opponent's return. This lack of preparation for whatever comes next is an infuriatingly common error among weekenders. They rely totally on blind improvisation. It's the same as playing chess one move at a time, never thinking further ahead. The only way you'll win is by a miracle. Learn to have your shot play your opponent.

COURT 25. I've noticed this girl here on several occasions. What red-blooded American male wouldn't? She has lots of ability, plays a sound, steady game, and yet she's never going to be a real winner. Losing doesn't bother her enough. Once I walked over after she'd lost a close match—thinking I might be able to console her, you know, some women get deeply depressed when they lose—but she wasn't even slightly upset. "What difference does it make?" she said with a shrug. "Seven-five is a respectable score to lose by." I'd heard that sentiment before, of course, but I've never quite been able to get used to it. The idea of a "respectable score to lose by" strikes a serious tennis player as absurd; the only respectable scores are those you win by. And if there were such a thing, it would not be 7–5. That's a *terrible* score to lose by. It suggests that your ability is about equal to your opponent's but that possibly you failed to make that little extra effort that could have turned defeat into victory. In a way, 6–0 is a more respectable loss; no shame attaches to being outclassed.

COURT 26. There's a real old-timer for you—he must be seventy-five. Notice how he holds his racket. That's known as a western grip. See how he uses the same side of the strings for hitting both forehand and backhand shots? You don't see many tennis players use that grip these days. It's great for hitting high strokes but lousy for the low ones—you're ruined, the way the game is played today. Unless you've been using it for sixty years or so, my advice is to let the western grip alone. The eastern grip—sometimes known as the "shake hands" grip—is much better suited to the fast, modern game. Ninety-eight per cent of the players at Forest Hills this year used it.

COURT 27. I wonder what this woman thinks she's playing— croquet? Look how her racket hangs down. The head almost touches the ground. And she's standing at the net, no less. She has no chance at all to make a decent return of a ball that comes her way with any speed. She'll be lucky, in fact, if she gets her racket up fast enough to protect her pretty face. Keep your racket ready.

COURT 28. An outfielder in baseball can make a good play going backwards; the ball is hit deep, he turns toward the fence, drifts under it, and takes it over his shoulder. That youngster in the far court reminds me of an outfielder, the way he chases lobs. He hasn't returned one yet. His failure nicely illustrates one difference between the sports. In baseball, just catching the ball will sometimes end the play; in tennis, you must always hit it back again. And to hit it while you're moving away from the net is a guarantee that the shot will be a dud. What this youngster should do is to beat the ball to the base line, turn around, and move in again to meet it. Your weight should always be moving toward the net when you hit a tennis ball.

COURT 29. That short fellow confronted with the powerful serve doesn't quite know what to do about it. Consequently, he's making the common mistake of attempting to do too much. He's risking tricky placements on his return of service, and also trying to put heavy spin on it. As you see, he's not having much luck. The best way to cope with a blistering serve is to settle for getting it back. That's all you should try to accomplish. Grip your racket firmly and just block the ball with it. It isn't even necessary to swing. Already the serve carries more than enough pace to send it back over the net. Resist the temptation, when your opponent's serve is flashy, to make your return flashy too. The answer to flamboyance is steadiness.

COURT 30. Joe Muscles here seems to think that since he's permitted two serves, he can afford to waste the first one showing off with. He's trying to impress those two blondes over there. So he smashes the ball with every ounce of his strength, sends it over the net with the speed of a bullet, than flexes his biceps, awaits the "oohs" and "aahs"—and prepares to hit again. The first serve, of course, was out of the court. When he hits the ball that hard, he can't control it. So now comes the second one, a little pitty-pat effort, because this time he has to get the ball in. His opponent, who has been calmly awaiting its arrival, puts it away with a moderately paced forehand that gives him point, game, set, and match. He walks off the court with a blonde on each arm. Girls prefer winners to show-offs.

Chapter 3

MINI-COURSE IN TENNIS FUNDAMENTALS

WEEKEND PLAYERS begin to make errors the minute they pick up a tennis racket—often with an incorrect grip. Laziness, impatience, and poor concentration can properly be blamed for many of their mistakes, and these are hard enough to overcome. But even worse are the errors they unknowingly commit —over and over and over again, eventually turning them into unbreakable habits—because they lack a thorough grasp of fundamentals.

To play tennis properly, you must know what you're doing. You must understand the sport's basic principles. You must know about grips and spins and stroke production and be aware of the game's general tactics. Most weekenders overestimate their knowledge of these things. Or if they do understand them, they don't show it on the court. In any case, a review of fundamentals never hurts. We might as well begin at the beginning—with the grip.

THE GRIP

I hope you have a tennis racket handy by your side, because you'll get much better insight into the points we'll be discussing if you actually try them out as we proceed. If you do have a racket, I'd like you to pick it up now. Cradle the throat gently in your left hand, if you will, holding the handle parallel to the ground with the strings facing an imaginary net—in other words, in position to hit a forehand. Now shake hands with the handle. Just wrap your fingers and thumb around it. Take a comfortably firm but not vice-tight hold, with the butt end extending past the heel of your hand just a little bit. Keep your wrist straight, as if you had a splint on it. Congratulations. You have learned the eastern grip. This is the grip most commonly used today by the world's leading players and the one I personally recommend. Notice that the racket face is on the same plane as your palm. This allows you to swing it like a natural extension of your arm, with maximum power and control.

Okay, now we're ready for the backhand grip—there are really two eastern grips for hitting ground strokes. To show you why you can't use the forehand grip for backhands, I'd like you to reach your right hand across your body in whatever way seems to you most natural. Observe what happens to your palm. It tends to roll over and face downward, doesn't it? That's because of the way your arm's constructed. This is the position your hand will assume when you're hitting a backhand drive. Unless you want your racket head to face the ground too (you don't), you must compensate by shifting your grip. Rotate your hand to the left around the handle about a one-quarter turn or slightly less—somewhere between 45 and 90 degrees, whatever it takes to make your right arm feel comfortable and keep the racket head facing the net. Forehands are hit with one side of the strings, backhands with the other, of course. Moving from the forehand to the backhand position, your left hand guides the racket by cradling its throat and holds the strings perpendicular to the ground. Simultaneously, your grip shifts on the handle. Don't think of the racket as rotating within your hand. That isn't the way it happens. Your right hand is what does the rotating. Some players—roughly half, I'd guess—make a second modification for backhands. Rather than curling their thumb around the handle, as you always should do for a forehand shot—you should actually make your thumb touch one of your fingers—they extend it out straight along the backside of the handle for additional support and control. Either way is acceptable. Try both and take your pick.

Now you know the proper grips for executing ground strokes, but what happens when you advance to the net? The action is too fast there to shift the grip between shots; you simply don't have time. So you have to choose a favorite and stick with it. A few players still prefer the forehand grip at net, but the most popular choice among better players is the eastern backhand grip. Either one is likely to feel strange at first—hitting a forehand volley with a backhand grip, for instance—but with practice you'll begin to get used to it.

Or else you can compromise with the continental grip (also known as the eastern service grip, because it's the one most frequently used in serving), which is somewhere in between. Pick up your racket in an eastern forehand grip, then rotate your hand to the left around the handle about one-sixth revolution. Now you're using a continental grip. If that's all you shift to hit backhands, it's the same as your backhand grip. Some tennis players use *only* the continental grip, even for forehand drives; they never have to shift their hand at all. Despite this advantage, I still prefer the eastern grip for the power and control it provides. The continental grip on the forehand dictates a strong wrist.

Maybe you'd like to know what the western grip is. You might have heard older players mention it. Years ago, top tennis stars like Little Bill Johnston (in deference to Big Bill, who of course was Bill Tilden) used the western grip with considerable success. It's especially good for returning high shots. But then as the game began to get faster, the western grip virtually passed out of use because fast, low shots are hard to manage with it. Today you seldom see it any more. But if you're curious, here's how the thing works. Once again, hold your racket in an eastern forehand grip. Rotate your hand a one-quarter turn to the *right*—the opposite direction from the eastern backhand grip—so that your palm is facing up when you hit forehands. That's all there is to it. You're using a western grip. You hit forehands and backhands with the same side of the strings, which means waving the racket in front of your face as if it were a Japanese fan. Now that you know what it is, you're free to forget it.

Whichever grip you use, in whatever circumstances, tighten your hold before the moment of impact and always relax your hand between shots. Otherwise, you're going to get arm cramps.

Now let's talk a little bit about putting "stuff" on the ball.

Spins

I hate to make mention of golfers again, but they're such good bad examples I can't help it. The terminology they use to describe spins, for example. Actually, I can't understand why golf shots aren't all straight—I mean, with the ball being stationary and all. But I notice just from watching them drive off the tee that golfers almost never hit straight shots. Half the time the drive curves off to the left, in which case the golfer (I'm assuming he's right-handed) scowls at his club, as if *it* were to blame, and complains about hitting a "hook." Other times it tails off in the opposite direction and he refers to it in his curses as a "slice." A slice? To the right? Well, leave it to golfers to get everything all mixed up.

Maybe it's because of the language of the links that so many weekend tennis players are so frequently confused by the terminology (and the purpose) of spins. Let's see if we can straighten things out.

In tennis, a slice is like a curve ball in baseball; if you're right-handed, it breaks to your left as you deliver it, to your right-handed opponent's forehand side. It moves in the direction of your follow-through, both before and after it bounces. Pretend that as you see the ball approaching through the air, it's numbered like the face of a clock. By striking it on the right side, in the three-o'clock position, hitting through it with a right-to-left snap, while at the same time propelling it in a forward direction, you can give a ball the same kind of spin with a racket that a curve-ball pitcher imparts with his wrist. If you were above it looking down, you'd see it spinning counterclockwise. This is what tennis players call a slice.

The closest thing in tennis to what *golfers* call a slice is the way the American twist serve bounces. We'll talk about the different ways of serving later on. Suffice it to say here that when you deliver an American twist, your racket meets the ball at about the ten-o'clock position, spinning it with a decided snap of the wrist. It curves the same direction as the slice does through the air, though not to so great a degree. But when it bounces, the twist alters course; it kicks off sharply to the server's right and bounds high—toward the receiver's backhand side and over his left shoulder—sometimes his most vulnerable spot.

The twist spin is restricted to the service, of course, because you can't hit a moving ball that way; even serving, you sometimes feel like a contortionist. A slice, though, can be used on many other occasions—any time you can give the ball a sidewise spinning motion. But relatively few returns should be sliced. Instead, give them topspin or underspin.

To understand the behavior of a ball that carries topspin (or overspin, the terms are synonymous), think of it as turning forward somersaults. Essentially, that's what it's doing. It's spinning in the same general direction as its flight path, which gives it extra quickness through the air and off the ground and tends to keep it fast and elusive. Topspin is basically an attacking weapon. Many players put topspin on almost all their ground strokes. The technique takes time to master. While your arm is moving forward in the swing, simply keep your racket head lower than the ball, then hit it with a slight upward movement. About nine-tenths forward and one-tenth upward is how you might analyze the stroke.

The opposite motion imparts backspin (or underspin). You keep your racket head higher than the ball during the swing, then hit with a slight chopping movement. Undercutting the ball, it's sometimes called. The racket face is angled like the plane of an ax, with the strings facing upward and over the net, so that it hits down on the underside of the ball. (For topspin, naturally, this tilt is reversed; the racket strings are angled toward the ground a few degrees.) Backspin is basically a defensive device, especially well suited to drop shots and dinks but also used (sparingly) for strokes hit with more pace.

Spin Gives Control

Contrary to what many weekend players believe, a "flat" ball is more difficult to control than one that carries topspin or backspin—assuming, of course, that you've practiced enough spin shots to be familiar with the way they travel. You can hit a spin shot harder without sending it out of bounds because of the natural way a spin shot curves downward. Flat shots tend to sail. Cannonball serves, which are basically flat, are almost never used by top players especially for second services; when you *have* to get the ball in, the odds suggest a spin serve—either a slice or an American twist. Pancho Gonzales, who had one of the hardest serves in history, once told me that he never hit a serve without *some* spin. When he was missing with his serve, he added spin for more control; as his control returned, he took off some of the spin for greater speed.

Another good reason for putting spin on your shots is that a spinning ball is tricky to return. It can twist right off your opponent's racket unless his stroke is perfectly timed. He must understand the spin. Also, if he's planning a spin shot of his own, yours could easily sabotage his effort. If he tries to put backspin on a ball *you've* given backspin, for instance, he risks sending it straight up in the air. Even if he knows how to get around this danger—by waiting until the ball reaches the top of its bounce, where the spin effect lessens, and *then* hitting it —you've given yourself lots of time to get ready.

Learning to hit strokes with either topspin *or* backspin, with an occasional slice thrown in for good measure, and with a swing that successfully disguises the intent, should be every tennis player's desire. Then you can keep your opponent forever off stride by constantly changing pace—three forehands hit with topspin, say, then suddenly a fourth hit with backspin. If you're able to mix them up like that, your opponent is in for a hard afternoon.

Now let's talk about the various strokes. We can start with the most basic, the forehand drive.

Forehand

Much that applies to hitting good forehand drives applies equally to other tennis strokes. You should never, for example, take your eye off the ball until you see it strike the strings of your racket. Many players think it's necessary to look at the target. In the last split second before hitting the ball, they're watching their opponent's court. Don't. The court won't move when you aren't looking at it, and by this time you should know where it is. You don't have to see it to hit it. Keep your eyes glued to that ball.

Another basic rule, whether it's a forehand shot or not, is to meet the ball with your weight moving forward into the ball, toward the net. Position yourself where you'll be able to move in on the ball—just like an outfielder tries to do in baseball. It's easier to run forward than backward. Once a shot gets past you and has to be chased down, your return, if you return it, will inevitably be weak because you're moving away from the net. Move *in* on the ball whenever possible. And as you hit it, shift your weight from your back foot to your front—from right foot to left, for a forehand.

Your forehand should begin, like all shots in tennis, from the neutral "ready" position: You're facing the net with your racket straight in front of you, the fingers of your left hand cradling its throat, your right hand around it in an eastern forehand grip, its butt end aimed at your stomach; your body is relaxed and poised on your toes, knees relaxed, prepared to move in any direction.

Now here comes the ball—it's to your right, a forehand shot. (I'm assuming you're a right-handed tennis player, an assumption I'll continue through the book. Lefties will have to make the usual transpositions. This is only fair, because on the tennis court itself, circumstances usually favor the southpaw. Most of his opponents will be used to facing right-handed players and will often have a problem adjusting. A player who shows up with his left hand on the racket is plus-15 already.) You pivot on your right foot, cross over with your left (make your first step with whichever foot is farther from the ball), and move into what I think of as the batter's box. The best stance for hitting a forehand drive—or any other tennis stroke, as far as that goes—is exactly like a batter's stance in baseball. Your left side (for the forehand) faces the direction of flight. Your knees are slightly bent, your feet shoulder-width apart, and you're a comfortable hitting distance from the ball. The *instant* you can tell that the shot will be a forehand, you should move toward this position and initiate your backswing by letting your racket travel back with your right shoulder. At the same time, your left hand will extend out in front, serving as a counterbalance. Don't twist your shoulders any farther than your torso turns; an exaggerated wind-up costs you speed and control.

Now you have to decide where you want to aim the ball. For a cross-court return, you'll want to meet it out in front—approximately off your left toe. For a shot down the line, you can wait an instant longer and hit it when it's over home plate. Time your swing accordingly and disguise your intent as long as you possibly can. As your racket moves forward, keep it parallel to the ground at roughly the level of your waist. You want to hit all forehands waist-high. Obviously, if the ball is at the level of your chin, you have to move deeper in the court and let it fall. For low shots, bend your knees and get your waist down. Don't just stoop over and reach your racket head down. Lower your waist and your racket head will go with it.

At the moment of impact, your waist should be locked, your grip tight, your weight shifting forward. Then make a full, complete follow-through. Too many weekenders think a stroke is completed the instant they hit the ball. It isn't. The follow-through is extremely important. Let the racket swing freely in an arc across your body until it's pointing up over your left shoulder. Then immediately move back into the "ready" position for whatever kind of shot might come next.

BACKHAND

The backhand employs the same principles as the forehand and theoretically is an easier and more powerful shot because you're swinging away from your body; the movement is a natural uncoiling. With a forehand, what you're doing is mostly pushing the racket rather than releasing a cocked tension. Yet few weekend players feel at home with the backhand. They use the stroke only when they're forced to. They run around the ball and hit a forehand shot rather than standing still and using a backhand. They're accustomed to hitting baseballs and golf balls from the right side, and of course they also throw from that side; to hit a backhand from the "wrong" side seems unnatural.

But in tennis it isn't the wrong side at all. The difference is that those other sports use two-handed grips. Essentially, it's a case of one arm supplying the power and the other providing guidance. And notice that the power arm is always the one in front. This is true in any sport. A golfer swings right-handed because that hand has finer touch, not because his right arm is stronger; it isn't. A golfer's left arm is stronger. The same goes for a long-ball hitter in baseball; his front arm, the one nearest the pitcher, is the one that gives him power. In tennis, though, where you swing with a one-handed grip, the same arm serves both of these functions; it has better touch and also greater strength. This explains why top tennis players who also play golf usually swing from the opposite side. If they're right-handed tennis players, they're left-handed golfers. The reason is that they want to have their power arm in front, the position where it always does most good. (Maybe I shouldn't reveal this in print. Tennis players like to have fun teasing golfers by telling them their game is so ridiculously easy that the only challenge is to play it left-handed—and then doing so.)

Anyhow, when you're hitting a backhand in tennis, your power arm is in its strongest position. Through practice, you should learn to knock the cover off the ball. It isn't mere coincidence that Don Budge and Rod Laver, the only two players ever to win the Grand Slam, both capitalized on the awesome potential of the backhand and made it their strongest stroke. (They're also both redheads, but I'm not sure that matters.)

As you step into the imaginary batter's box for a backhand, stand a little closer to home plate than for a forehand; you have to reach your arm across your body as you put the racket in the hitting position. Shift your grip during the backswing, while your left hand is guiding the racket, and hold your elbow in close until you start your forward motion. Then straighten it out as you swing—the same as you should do for a forehand. Weekend players have a tendency, in hitting backhands, to start with their racket head high and stroke down. This results in giving it side and backspin. No wonder they regard it as primarily a defensive stroke; they give it a defensive spin. But no law says they have to. It's better, in fact, to hit a backhand with topspin. Keep the racket head lower than the ball and hit up and over. Topspin adds pace, remember.

Backhands must be hit a little earlier than forehands—about one foot in front of your right toe for a cross-court, and about even with that toe for a shot down the line. If you wait until it reaches the home-plate position, you'll have to hit the ball with a cramped swing.

As with the forehand, you should bend your knees to get your waist down for low backhands, and don't make the mistake so many players do of just punching at backhand returns. Use a full, easy follow-through and let it run its course.

So much for the forehand and backhand drives, the so-called ground strokes of tennis. These strokes serve as the foundation of your game. You'll use them more often than all other strokes put together. A beginner should practice them hour after hour, grooving his swing and getting comfortable with the rhythm, before moving on to the next stroke, the lob.

THE LOB

The lob is by far the most neglected stroke in tennis, especially among weekend players. They often go a whole set without lobbing even once. And when they do lob, it's almost always defensively. They underestimate the possibilities of the stroke.

The primary purpose of a defensive lob is to allow yourself a little extra time to recover when you're caught in a poor position. Say your opponent has pulled you off the court with a sharply angled drive. To get back where you belong, you hit a high deep lob, usually cross-court because that gives you more distance. A touch of backspin, by slowing its flight, will help too. You want to send it up there as high as you can without losing control of where it lands. Good players can manage thirty feet. The more altitude it has, the more time it provides you in which to return to position.

With an offensive lob, you can win a point outright. Spring it when your opponent is too close to the net. Just arch the ball over his head. Again, you want to keep it just as deep as you can. Always try to keep a lob deep. But this time the trajectory should be relatively low. Use topspin if you think you can manage it. You're not doing the running now, the other guy is. Don't give him time to catch up to it. At its apex, an offensive lob might be ten feet off the ground, just high enough to keep it out of reach. Naturally, you want an offensive lob to come as a surprise. If you tip it off, it probably won't work. Start your swing as you would for a forehand drive (or backhand drive if the lob is a backhand), then just poke it up there at the very last instant and use an abbreviated follow-through. The best way to protect yourself from a lob attack, of course, is not to be caught with your nose over the net. Also, give your approach shot more depth and greater pace; your opponent will have trouble getting a good offensive lob off when the ball carries reasonable speed and lands deep.

In addition to the offensive and defensive lobs, there's a third kind we might call the infuriating lob. This one you use to give the other guy fits with when the sun's in his eyes or the wind is playing tricks or to make him look up when it's sprinkling. All's fair in love, war, and tennis.

DROP SHOTS

Are you familiar with the terms "change-up" or "pulling the string," in the sense in which baseball pitchers use them? Or "junk pitch" or "backbreaker" or "taking something off it"? Mention these phrases around a guy who swings for fences and he'll give you a dirty look and grind his teeth.

Tennis players who excel at the "big" game are that way. They'd like to hit at nothing but fast balls all the time—the kind they can rip right back at you. It annoys them when a shot is hit at less than full power, and little bloopers nearly drive them up the wall. Don Budge has nothing but contempt for the drop shot. He calls it a "nothing ball." When I played him, you can bet he saw some drop shots.

A drop shot is a soft stroke hit delicately with or without backspin that should land as close as possible to the net. But don't use *severe* backspin because your motion will give it away; you want to keep a drop shot well disguised. Caress the shot. If your opponent is a slugger and you've caught him playing deep, he'll come racing toward the net in frustration. If he manages to reach the ball with his racket at all, he'll be forced to hit up—which means his shot won't have much pace. Then you hit the other stroke he fiercely hates—the lob—and keep him running back and forth between the net and the base line getting angrier and more exhausted every trip. Be careful, though, that you don't put the ball where he can smash it. You might be picking fuzz off your molars.

"Chop," "chip," and "dink" are other terms you might have heard for shots aimed near the net with backspin. Chop and chip are synonymous; the words are interchangeable. Under either name, the stroke is a long-distance drop shot. You should hit a drop shot while standing near the net; you hit it softly, with just a minimum of follow-through. For a chop, which is often used for the return of service, you'll be hitting from a deeper position; therefore, use a little more follow-through (though less than you would for a drive). Start with the racket about as high as your shoulder, then hit down and through the ball to give it some backspin. Do what the name suggests: chop it.

"Dink" is a general term for any kind of spin shot plopped softly over the net. Two rules to keep in mind about this kind of stroke are not to overdo it (you'll lose the element of surprise) and not to hit dinks from deep in the court. They'll have too far to travel and they're moving too slowly; your opponent will be able to move into the net and put them away with a volley—which is the next stroke up for discussion.

THE VOLLEY

Drop shots and dink shots—slow shots in general—are relatively rare in tennis. Usually when you volley, you're standing at the net and the ball is coming at you very fast. You may barely have time to stick your racket up in front of it. But that's okay, that's all you *have* to do. The speed the ball arrives with is enough to send it back; you only have to change its direction. For this, you don't need a big wind-up or mighty swing. In fact, you don't really need any swing to volley. It's more like catching a ball than hitting it. Imagine your racket as a first baseman's glove and just hold it where the ball will run into it. If time allows, you can give the ball a short, punching motion, the way a boxer might deliver a jab. But your racket should travel less than a foot. Avoid the mistake so common among weekenders of volleying with big roundhouse swings. Sure, you want the volley to win the point outright, but a big swing just diminishes your chances. While you're winding up, the ball zips right past you. If you don't have time at net to shift your grip (and you don't), you certainly don't have time for a full backswing. Keep your grip and wrist firm.

Volley if at all possible from a point above the net cord so your shot can follow a straight downward path; that's the way you win a point outright. If you let the ball drop lower than the net cord before striking it, you'll be forced to play defensively and hit up.

Many players, especially women, act afraid at the net. They volley at arm's-length distance. Their control would be much better if they hit from closer range—a distance of a foot or two, let's say. Don't be bullied by fear at the net. Your self-protective reflexes are probably quicker than you think, and the face of your racket is big. All you have to do is stick it in front of you.

By definition, a volley never touches the ground; you return it before it bounces. This makes the "half volley" an obvious misnomer, because a half volley *does* touch the ground. It's like a pickup in baseball, or like trapping the ball, when you barely miss catching it on the fly. The half volley is perhaps the most difficult shot in tennis and also the most defensive. By staying out of no mans' land—the middle of the court—you can avoid having to make it at all.

THE OVERHEAD

Do you know why so many weekend players flub so many overhead shots? Because they take too big a backswing. They've been told that an overhead is much like a serve—as in many ways it is, same grip, same kind of motion—and they're accustomed to giving their serve a big wind-up. They want desperately to put their full strength behind it, go for broke. That attitude is fine, the smash should be a killer, but they're ignoring an important distinction. When you serve, you're hitting a motionless ball. At the top of the toss, it's neither rising nor falling, just suspended there waiting to be slugged. It might as well be sitting on a tee. But the target for an overhead is your opponent's falling lob shot, and a descending ball is difficult to time. A big backswing will almost surely throw you off.

Imagine that you're hammering a nail into the wall as high as you can comfortably reach. That's the way you want to hit an overhead—hard but with a short swing so you don't crush your thumb. Keep your eye on the ball until the instant you hit it, but do *not* follow its flight off your racket. Instead, keep looking at the position of impact, the way a golfer watches the tee after he drives. That's another grave error weekend players often make. Before they hit an overhead, and sometimes *while* they're hitting it, they look to see where their opponent is standing—trying to pick out a target. Then they hit the ball off-center and blow the shot. Forget your opponent. Where he's standing doesn't matter. If you hit the ball solidly and land it deep in the court, the odds are very good you'll have a winner. Don't be afraid to aim deep with an overhead. Three times more errors come from hitting overheads into the net than from hitting them over the base line.

Another reason why overheads are so often botched up is that few players practice the shot. They never learn to time a falling ball. But even those who work at it for hour after hour may occasionally be unable to get the knack. One of these people was none other than Bill Tilden, considered by some authorities the best player who ever lived. Overheads gave Tilden all sorts of trouble. Especially when the sun angle or a strong wind made things worse, he often chose to let the ball bounce and hit a ground stroke. Maybe that's your solution if you simply can*not* hit overheads. But I urge you not to give up too soon. You'll be sacrificing the use of a powerful weapon that can win you a great many points. And who knows? If you keep practicing, you may learn to hit overheads better than Tilden himself. Lay your overhead simple, neat, and tidy—and hit 'em where they ain't.

Now we come to what is basically a variation of the over-head—the serve, the most important stroke in tennis.

THE SERVE

The secret to a good serve is a smooth, unhurried swing. Basically, it's an overhand throwing motion. Pretend you're Willie Mays making a long throw to the plate, but instead of throwing a ball, you're throwing your racket. The ball enters the equation later on. I often tell players having trouble with their serve to lay the ball down for a while. Just concentrate on the swing your right arm makes.

Even before the swing, though, you must assume the proper stance. Stand behind the base line about two feet from the center mark, left or right depending on which court you want to hit to. Put your left foot at a 45-degree angle with the base line, not touching it but just slightly behind it. (If you touch it, you're guilty of a foot fault.) Then put your right foot parallel to the base line a comfortable distance behind your left—usually about eighteen inches. Now you're ready to swing.

At this juncture, many instructors bewilder their students by dissecting and analyzing the many ingredients of the simple throwing motion of the serve. It's like those how-to-play-golf books where the elements of the swing are scrutinized for sixty-five pages. When the reader eventually steps up to the tee, his head's so full of worries about his various bones and joints— how his knees should be turned, where his elbows belong, the proper position for his shoulders and hips—that he succeeds only in flubbing the shot. My advice is to ignore these distracting complexities and just concentrate on throwing the racket over the net. Everyone presumably knows how to throw overhand, and that's the kind of motion you should serve with. If a beat-up old tennis racket happens to be handy, literally throw it over the net. If not, just pretend that you're doing so.

The racket should land in your opponent's service court, approximately where you'd want to have the ball land.

When you've done this a few times, pick up a ball. The toss is a critical part of the serve. In every other tennis stroke, you're forced to chase the ball; its speed and position dictate your swing. Only in the serve can you control every factor, and good players always make the most of this advantage by perfecting a well-controlled toss. To serve well, you *must* have a smooth, controlled toss. If it flies every which way, you'll be chasing it with your racket, and you might as well be hitting a return shot.

A good toss is characterized by economy of motion. Hold the ball in the fingertips of your left hand, palm up, no lower than the level of your waist. You don't need any more of a wind-up. Then lift the ball in front of you—by which I mean don't throw it—as high as your left arm can easily extend, and release it so it rises just a few feet farther, to the highest point your racket will comfortably reach. That's where the ball should stop its ascent, pause briefly before falling, and—crunch!—that's when you hit it.

Proper timing of the toss takes a great deal of practice. The hardest part is to co-ordinate it with the swing of the racket so that the ball is suspended exactly where you want it precisely when the racket arrives there. It has to be a perfect rendezvous, as the astronauts might phrase it.

For either a cannonball serve or a slice, this rendezvous spot should be about an arm's length in front of you—directly toward the net for the cannonball delivery, a little to your right for the slice. The cannonball is used almost exclusively as a first serve. Because it's "flat," it's the hardest type of service to control, too risky to attempt for second serves. For a hard, flat cannonball, hit the ball near dead center, holding your racket in an eastern forehand grip. It's the equivalent of the high, hard fastball in baseball. The follow-through, like that of a baseball pitcher, is down and across your body. Your right foot swings forward as you make the delivery, and the racket ends up low and to your left.

For a spin serve—either a slice or an American twist—hold the racket in an eastern backhand grip, or in the eastern service (continental) grip. Trial and error will tell you which works best. For a slice, hit the ball at about its three-o'clock position, stroking it in a right-to-left direction. Snap your wrist to give it the spin. The follow-through is like that for the cannonball. The slice is the easiest kind of delivery to control, and you can use it for either first or second serves.

The American twist is harder to get the knack of. It helps if you're young and agile. You toss the ball straight up over your head, arch your back, swing your racket way behind your head, then reach under and over the ball and, with a snap of your wrist, hit it at about the ten-o'clock position. The follow-through is down and to your *right* side this time. It sounds a bit awkward, and indeed it often is. The best way to learn the American twist is to watch someone who does it properly, then copy him. The twist is usually used for second serves. With the correct motion and spin it takes a very wicked bounce toward your opponent's backhand side. Its spinning motion makes it fairly easy to control once you get the feel of the thing.

Whatever type of serve you use, there are basic rules to follow. First of all, get the serve in. Two thirds of your first serves—at *least* two thirds—and all of your second serves should land in the proper service court. More than one double fault per set is too many.

The second rule is to hit the serve deep. Use it to take the initiative and keep your opponent on the defensive.

Rule number three is to avoid predictable patterns. Do not, for example, make every first serve a cannonball to your opponent's forehand, then follow it each time with a slice serve to his backhand. Vary them as to type, speed, placement, and sequence, so that he never knows what's coming next.

And avoid the common weekend player's mistake of making the first serve and the second vastly different—an atomic bomb followed by a love pat. Practice until you can get most of your first serves in, and learn to put controlled pace on your second serves.

TACTICS

The variety of tactics used in tennis is endless. Bruce Old and I collaborated to write two books on the subject—*The Game of Singles in Tennis* and *The Game of Doubles in Tennis*—and barely scratched the surface. If you're an advanced player, you might benefit from reading them. I review them myself before I play a big match. But I've found that many weekenders are confused and discouraged by a detailed analysis of strategy. They'd be better off if they concentrated on a few basic rules that underlie a sound, winning game. Here they are:

◄ Above all, get the ball back. You can't lose on a shot you return. Of course, that sounds obvious—maybe even simple-minded—but a great many players forget it. Or else they don't realize that when the point is finally tallied, not losing is the same thing as winning. They're victims of the feeling that they don't *deserve* to win a point when all they do is stubbornly keep hitting the ball back until the other guy makes a mistake; they think they ought to *earn* the point through more flamboyant tactics. Which is precisely why about four times more points are lost than won—because too many players try shots they lack the skill for. They overextend themselves. Attempting a spectacular placement that misses, rather than settling for a safe return, will win you no medals for valor. You've failed at your primary job: to get the ball back. Naturally, it's always nice to put pace on a shot and to land it in an area your opponent can't reach, but even if your return is just a poorly placed sitter, he'll frequently manage to flub it. But not unless you give him that chance.

◄ Make your opponent hit up. By "up" I mean from a point below the top of the net. He can't possibly send the ball back on a straight line from that position. If he returns it, he'll have to arch it over the net, which means it will carry reduced pace. Conversely, on your own returns, hit down whenever possible. Letting the ball fall lower than the level of the net cord when you could just as easily have hit it sooner in its descent is to toss a big advantage out the window. The higher the ball's position when you meet it with your racket, the better angle you enjoy for line drives.

◄ Adopt an attitude of cautious aggressiveness. The two words are not contradictory. A tennis player is simultaneously on offense and defense, and the trick is to achieve the right balance. The unrestrained aggressor who mounts wild-eyed attacks is a pretty good bet to have his brains beaten out except when his opponent is the opposite extreme, the cringer who never advances to the net. Good players are continuously anxious to attack, but unwilling to do so foolishly. They keep pressing their opponent, moving him around, discouraging him from launching an attack of his own, all the while looking for a moment of vulnerability when they can instantly move in for the kill. In other words, work patiently for a *good* opening, then take it.

◄ Exploit your opponent's weaknesses. Bill Tilden considered it psychologically shrewd to challenge a player's strength. Matched against someone with a formidable backhand, Tilden might deliberately keep hitting to the backhand and ignore his more vulnerable spots. His theory was that when you show a guy his best just ain't good enough, you shatter his confidence at the beginning of the match, and from that point on, you can coast. For Tilden, it worked; he had the skill to bring it off. For most weekend players, it won't. Playing against someone with a very strong backhand, you'd be wise to attack some other point— preferably wherever he's weakest. Not *all* the time, of course; you should vary your attack in order to keep him honest and guessing. But especially when a critical point is up for grabs, his weakness is your primary target.

◄ Return the ball at your earliest chance. As soon as it passes over the net is ideal. Your opponent won't have time to recover from his last shot before being forced to make the next one. If you're content to play every return from the base line . . . well, add up the distance the ball has to travel, just on your side of the net. Horizontally, it goes approximately twice the length of the court—from the net to your position, then back again. Since it bounces, there is also a vertical component, no less than the distance from the net cord to the ground, then up to whatever height you hit it at. That's quite a bit of traveling. It consumes enough time to give your opponent a good chance to get ready. But when you stand at the *net* and hit overheads and volleys, the ball stays on your side for only a split second before it's back in your opponent's court again. This is why gaining the net is so important, and when attained by proper attack, two thirds of all points are won there.

◄ Stay out of no man's land. Standing right smack dab in the middle of the court—roughly where the service line meets the half court line—is about the worst spot you can find yourself in. Unless you're a master of the low volley or half volley, your opponent will kill you by hitting at your feet. Play back near the base line or up at the net; never linger anywhere in between. Of course, you don't want to get *too* close to the net. If your nose is hanging over it, you're vulnerable to a lob. About six to nine feet back is ideal.

◄ Have a purpose for every shot. Too many players are content to hit the ball back without trying to accomplish anything specific beyond that. They aren't going to win very often. Every shot should have one of three purposes behind it, and you should decide which one it's to be. First, you can try to put it away for a winner—a purely attacking shot. Second, it might be an obvious save—a strictly defensive shot; you're trying to get out of trouble. Or third, it could be a maneuvering shot, an attempt to move your opponent around, invite errors, and press him toward an opening. Don't just react to what the other guy does. Whoever takes the initiative usually wins.

◄ If you're losing, change tactics; if you're winning, plug away. Presumably, you began the match with a certain game plan in mind. By all means give it a chance. But don't stubbornly insist on sticking with it if it fails. Try something else instead. After all, what can you lose? On the other hand, if the plan works, don't abandon it. Too many players get cute when they're ahead. They whimsically switch tactics, sacrifice their momentum, and let the other guy get out from underneath. Given a second life, he frequently wins.

◄ When in doubt, hit deep and in the corner. In doubles, your best bet is down the middle (partly because of the question of which player should return it), but in singles the corners are better. A possible exception is when you're hitting an approach shot; hitting it down the middle reduces the angle available for an opponent's passing shot.

◄ Eliminate all waste motion. "In anything at all, perfection is finally attained not when there is no longer anything to add, but when there is no longer anything to take away." The man who made that statement, Antoine de Saint Exupéry, happened to be talking about airplane design, but it could just as well have been tennis, because the same rule applies: whatever you don't need is an encumbrance. It opens the door for errors. Every good tennis player knows the value of economy. His backswing is contained, and his wind-up before serving is never exaggerated. He doesn't start his toss around his ankles somewhere and throw it up twenty-five feet. In going to the net, he pursues a direct course. In moving into position to make a return, he always goes straight to the imaginary batter's box; he doesn't run parallel to the net to meet the ball, then turn sharply and accompany it to the base line. No move on the court should be superfluous.

◀ Prevent your opponent from playing the game he wants to. Your opponent plays the way you allow him to play. If you're matched against a slugger, give him nothing to slug; feed him soft shots and lobs and dinks. If he likes to play quickly, take your time between serves. Or if he enjoys a leisurely pace, speed it up. If you notice that he hits his best shots with a big backswing, add pace to your shots to make him shorten it. Keep him in the backcourt if he plays well at net. Whatever he does best, don't let him do it.

◀ Recognize that speed isn't everything. Control and deception are more important than velocity in making a good tennis shot. Top priority should be given to placement which wins a point outright or forces an error. Everything depends on hitting the ball where you want it. Next in importance is the element of surprise. Your opponent can't start running after a well-disguised shot until he actually sees it come off your racket. But if you telegraph your intent, he'll get a two-step head start. And no player can put enough speed on the ball to overcome a two-step handicap.

◀ Always hold something in reserve. Tennis matches are frequently long and demanding, and it doesn't pay to spend yourself early. Try to conserve your strength. One way is by getting your first service in, so you won't have to duplicate the effort; in the course of a match, it adds up. Also, you should try to keep some extra speed in hand. If most of your serves are only three-quarter speed, for instance, you have a good chance of catching your opponent off guard when you suddenly pull out all the stops. Similarly, if you think you see a weakness in his game, you might postpone attacking it until later in the match when you have to win a critical point.

◄ Constantly vary your game. Some players hit nothing but lobs throughout one point, then nothing but drives in the next point. That isn't the right kind of variety. No style would be easier to beat. *Within* every point you should instill some variety —and not just by using different strokes. Vary their position, and the pace you put on them, and the type and amount of their spin. If possible, your opponent should never know what's coming next.

◄ Play within the limits of your ability. In a match, your objective should always be to win. It isn't a practice session. Use only those shots you feel you can manage and avoid taking foolish risks with them. Aim no closer to the side lines than you can without missing. Until you've gotten the knack of the American twist, serve only spins with controlled speed in competition. If you can't play the net, stay back until you can. The way to win at tennis is by being consistent, and no one can be consistent outside his range of skills.

◄ Concentrate; plan ahead; *think*. If your mind tends to wander from the task at hand, you won't often win playing tennis. You simply *must* bear down, both mentally and physically, the whole time you're out there on the court. Like chess players, good tennis players plan several moves ahead; their opponent's anticipated response to a shot is an element in their decision to make it. Bad players, on the other hand, are constantly surprised. They stop in their tracks to watch every shot they make, sometimes pridefully, sometimes with dismay, but never giving the next one a thought. They alternate between inertia, just standing around watching, and desperation lunges and dives. Such a stop-and-go style marks a loser. Always assume that the ball will come back. As soon as you complete a tennis shot, anticipate the return and get ready.

Chapter 4

MINI-COURSE, SECOND SEMESTER: PLAYING DOUBLES

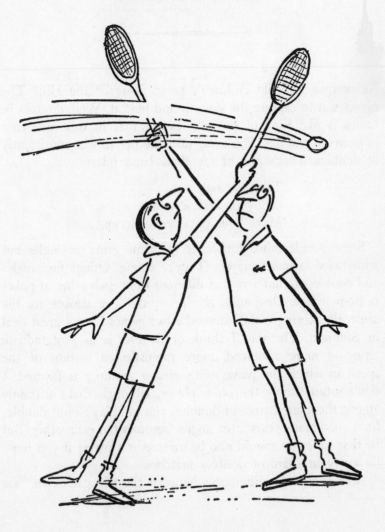

REMEMBER THE old children's game, King of the Hill? The object was to capture the summit and hold it. Well, doubles in tennis is like King of the Hill except that in this case your objective is the net. You *must* take the net to win consistently at doubles. That's one of my three basic rules:

> Take the net.
> Get your first serve in.
> Make your opponents hit up.

Some people think doubles is the same game as singles but with twice as many players. They're wrong. Others say singles and doubles are unrelated, as different from each other as poker is from bridge. Obviously, *they're* wrong. The strokes are the same, the scoring is the same—the two games have a great deal in common. The way I think of doubles is as postgraduate tennis—a more advanced, more sophisticated version of the sport, in which the player with greater maturity is favored. I don't mean simply the *older* player, although that's certainly among the many virtues of doubles: you can play all-out doubles for a good many years after singles becomes too exhausting. But by that time you should also be mature as a player if you hope to win your share of doubles matches.

Let's review the differences between the two games and see

what shifts of emphasis are called for when you switch from singles to doubles.

STROKES. Both games use the same basic strokes, of course, but doubles puts more emphasis on net play, overheads, and volleys and less on forehand and backhand drives, the so-called ground strokes of tennis. Ground strokes are reduced to an absolute minimum. In a match between two top doubles teams, the only ground strokes will be in the returns of service. After that, it's all volleys, lobs, and overheads—or it should be.

COURT POSITION. Gaining the net is crucial in doubles, much more important than in singles competition, and you should get there just as fast as you can—when you're serving, by following your serve in. In singles, it's advisable *not* to follow your serve in unless you're an accomplished volleyer. But in doubles, where you're covering a smaller portion of the court, the percentages swing the other way. By staying near the base line you give your opponents a big edge. Excluding the service and return of service, which obviously *must* be hit from the backcourt, fully 80 per cent of all points in doubles are won at the net position. Rule one: Get to the net.

SERVICE. Getting your first serve in in doubles is even more important than it is in singles. This is because your opponent must play back to receive it. On your second serve, he'll stand closer and can reach the net more easily, which is exactly what you don't want him to do. *At least* 80 per cent of your first serves should be in. This means, in a typical six-point game, no one faulted serve. Not double fault, mind you; one fault. You should never, never double fault in doubles. Nor should you attempt many aces or use your cannonball delivery. In doubles, every serve should carry spin. The American twist is the most advanced and best delivery—not only because a spin serve is more easily controlled but because a spinning ball moves more slowly through the air, allowing you more time to follow it to net. The difference between an American twist and a cannonball in this respect—assuming that both are hit deep, as they should be—is approximately three steps. That's a very big difference indeed. Even "big-game" players with blistering serves —the stalwarts of our 1969 Davis Cup team, Arthur Ashe and Stan Smith, could serve as examples—seldom serve with full power in doubles. The best doubles players serve with three-quarter speed and concentrate on accurate placement. Only on rare occasions, to surprise your opponent, should you pull out all the stops with a cannonball. The majority of your serves should be aimed at the receiver's backhand, but a smaller majority in doubles than in singles. Serving wide to the forehand is a good alternative in doubles. Get your first serve in—an excellent motto.

RETURN OF SERVICE. This is undoubtedly the hardest shot in doubles and probably the most important. A team returning well and closing into the net is in an excellent position to break serve. Holding serve (which means the server's team wins that particular game) is much easier in doubles than in singles. In only one game out of eight is there a service break in doubles, so the receiver has his work cut out for him. That fundamental fact gives the game its basic pattern, which was never stated more aptly than by George Lott, Jr., one of the finest doubles players in history. "Doubles," he said, "is mainly a matter of getting a service break, and then holding on for dear life." To get that vital break, you need a strong return of service. It must steal the initiative from the serving team and put them in a defensive position—a lob return, perhaps, that keeps the server in the backcourt while the receiver and his partner can capture the net, or a low dink that forces the server to hit up. Managing such returns off a difficult service is a tough job made tougher by discouraging odds, but in doubles it's the only way to win. Yet you mustn't attempt too much with your return of service. The first aim, as always, is to make sure you get the ball back. Force the other team to win the point, don't give it to them. Hit at their feet forcing them to volley up.

TACTICS. In doubles, there are fewer angled shots than in singles. The rule is: When in doubt, hit low down the middle. Don't aim for the alleys unless you have a sure placement. Beyond that, the geometry of the game becomes involved. With four people, the complexities are enormously greater than they are with only two. The relationship of doubles to singles in tennis could be compared to the relationship between chess and checkers. The experienced player with the analytical mind is the one most likely to win. Court craft is more vital than stroke production. Power is subordinate to cunning and touch. Brains usually triumphs over brawn.

SPEED. A doubles match involves less running than singles, but the pace of the game itself is much faster—the speed at which the ball moves back and forth. All four players are often at the net, firing at each other at point-blank range. It's therefore less important to be fleet afoot in doubles than to have quick reflexes and good anticipation. You *must* be able to anticipate to win. You must think ahead, weigh your opponents' possible shots, "feel" which one is coming, and get a jump on it. You can't just stand there, as you sometimes can in singles, waiting to see what happens next. You must foresee every shot and respond to it instantly. A split-second delay and you're dead.

TEAMWORK. Many top tennis players are loners, individualists. They're much more successful at singles than doubles. Bill Tilden is undoubtedly the classic example. For all his accomplishments as a singles player, Tilden was never a world-beater at doubles. He dismissed it as a vastly inferior game and professed not to understand why players like myself actually prefer doubles to singles. "Probably," he said, "it's because they have to do less work, have a partner to blame for defeat and someone to listen to their gripes as they play." No wonder he was never a first-rate doubles player when his approach to the game was so negative. Certainly I never viewed *my* partners that way. They weren't out there so I'd have someone to blame for defeat or to listen to my gripes as I played. They were there to help me win, and often succeeded. Very few players in the history of the game have won more doubles matches than I have. Gardnar Mulloy and I, among dozens of other victories, won the U.S. men's doubles championship four separate times. No team has won it more often in this century. Margaret Osborne and I won the U.S. mixed doubles championship four *consecutive* times—a feat no other team has yet accomplished. I don't mean to brag. I'm just trying to point out here that I can speak with at least as much authority as Tilden on doubles and the teamwork it requires.

It isn't just two players on the same side of the net pooling their talents in a makeshift alliance and providing each other with a wailing wall. It has to be a genuine partnership, a true union in a common cause. What this demands, first of all, is compatible personalities. I don't mean that the partners must be mutual best friends, but they *do* have to get along well together. Squabbling doubles partners seldom win. Second, their attitudes toward the game should be similar. If one's a grim competitor and the other clowns around, trouble is in the offing. Third, they must be able—potentially, at least—to communicate almost intuitively. When Mulloy and I were playing and a shot came down the middle, there was no mix-up as to which of us would take it; we understood the workings of each other's minds so thoroughly that on the court we were like Siamese twins. Naturally, this condition wasn't accomplished overnight. It was the consequence of our playing together for thousands of hours. That's the fourth basic requirement for a good doubles team: the willingness to work long and hard together. Mulloy and I were unusual, and exceedingly lucky, in that we clicked as a doubles team almost at once. The very first tournament we played together, we won—and it was the U.S. championships at Forest Hills. But we were enormously better after a couple years together. By that time, we found we could surprise our opponents without simultaneously surprising each other—a good goal to aim for in a partnership. Fifth, the partners' styles of play should complement each other. To say that a playmaker should be paired with a slugger is perhaps an oversimplification, but that's how the best teams have been structured. I was the playmaker and Mulloy was the slugger. Boy, how he could powder a tennis ball. My job was to get him a suitable opening by maneuvering the opposition into making weak returns.

Who plays the left court and who plays the right? Normally, the partner with the greatest power—the slugger in most playmaker-slugger combinations—is assigned to the left court or "ad court" (so called because it's the service court when the score reaches ad; the right court, by the same reasoning, is also called the "deuce court"). He does *not* play the left court because his backhand is stronger; that's a popular misconception. The idea is to get that powerful overhead on lobs and high penetrating volleys hit down the middle, where the majority of them go in doubles matches. For the same reason, a player with a superior backhand (or a left-handed player whose strength is his forehand) might well be assigned to the *right* court.

Usually, in one partnership you keep the same sides. Playing with Mulloy, I always took the right court, as I also did later when Tony Trabert was my partner. But in all other instances, in both men's and mixed doubles, my customary position was the left side. (The man almost always takes the left side in mixed.) In those cases, I was deemed to have the stronger overhead.

But *where* in the left court, or the right, do you stand? There are four different answers, one for each player—the server, his partner, the receiver, and *his* partner. For simplicity, let's talk about the serving team first. Then we'll take up the receiving team separately.

In the earliest days of doubles competition, all four players stayed back near the base line; it was a game of long rallies, a duel of ground strokes. Then, in the early 1880s, the one-up-and-one-back formation appeared; the server stayed back but his partner played the net. Unfortunately, that system didn't work very well (nor does it work very well for those players who still use it, of whom there are a great number among club players and weekenders), so the parallel system was adopted. In this one, which is considered the most effective style today, both partners play the net side-by-side—or at least try to. First, of course, they have to get up there.

In singles, as we saw in the previous chapter, the server should stand close to the center mark, usually about two feet to the side of it. But in doubles he should station himself nine feet away—exactly halfway between the center mark and the doubles side line. Then he should follow each serve straight toward the net, precisely down the middle of the side he's assigned to, until he reaches the service line. By that time, he can usually anticipate the return, and change direction or continue straight ahead, whatever's called for. (We're assuming a standard serving formation, with the server's partner on the opposite side; we'll discuss unconventional systems in a minute.) He doesn't want to linger at the service line, of course; a good return of service would trap him in no man's land. (The odds are approximately eight to one that the return will be hit to the server, not his partner.) That's simply where he chooses his course to the net, which he then pursues at maximum speed.

Meanwhile, what is his partner up to? The server's partner should stand at the net position, anywhere from six feet to nine feet back, a little closer to the center line than to the side line—about eight feet from the center line, ten feet from the side line. His height, reach, and ability to go back under a lob may call for slight modifications in that position. Then he shifts slightly in the direction of the serve, and as he watches the receiver prepare for the return, he decides on his course of action. Unless he has to retreat to the backcourt for a lob, he has three different options open. He can move toward the center to meet a cross-court return, possibly poaching on his partner's court; he can hold his own position for a shot down the line —one way his opponent may "keep him honest" and minimize poaching; or he can fake a move but not follow through with it. In any case, he wants to conceal his true intentions until the receiver is fully committed to his shot. If he anticipates a cross-court return and starts too early, the receiver can easily hit behind him for a placement. In such a case, the receiver is said to "wrong foot" the server's partner; he catches him leaning in the wrong direction, with his weight distributed on his feet in such a way that he's unable to recover in time. Naturally, any fake move is deliberately premature, a temptation for the receiver to hit to a vacated spot that will no longer be vacated when the ball arrives. If your opponents never lob, crowd the net.

There are three distinct purposes for the serving team's maneuvers: To play the return of service; to get to the net; to keep the opposition off stride and on the defensive. Varying the formation sometimes helps.

Let's imagine, for instance, that the receiver has an excellent cross-court return of service. Rushing in, the server has been incapable of handling it, especially when he's serving from the left court, the ad court—in other words, when it's hit to his backhand. So the serving team switches to the "Australian" formation, known also as the "tandem" or "reverse" formation. The server's partner stays at the net but switches sides. He positions himself in front of the server rather than at the usual diagonal; both are on the left side of the center line now. A cross-court return will go directly at the net man, who presumably can volley it with comparative ease. But of course *his* side —the right side, in this case—is now open. So the server takes a diagonal path to the net in order to plug the hole. To cut down the distance he'll have to go to get there, he serves from near the center mark, just as he would in singles. From the other side—when the server is delivering from the right side—the Australian formation is usually less effective, primarily because the server must play a down-the-line return of service with his backhand while running toward the net. And hitting a good backhand on the run isn't easy.

An element of deception helps the serving team too. For example, they might line up in a standard formation, then make their switch after the ball is in play, after the receiver is committed to his shot. This tactic, a delayed Australian formation, which I introduced in 1953 as captain of the American Davis Cup team (I had the players practice it secretly in their rooms, with the result that the Australian team of Lew Hoad and Rex Hartwig was completely surprised when we sprung it on them), is sometimes called a "scissors" or "crossover." Conversely, they might stand in an Australian formation, then switch the other way after the serve. Properly disguised, and combined with good fakes in which the partners co-ordinate their deceptive movements, these shifts can drive the opposition crazy.

Essentially, these maneuvers are all prearranged poaches. The net man signals his partner in advance—with hand signs usually, or by shouting a code word—that he intends to invade the server's territory. The poached-upon partner then covers for him. In the course of play, other situations will arise when poaches will have to be improvised. One player takes a ball in his partner's domain because he enjoys a better shot at it. That's fine when it helps the team win that point, but be wary about poaching too much. Nobody likes playing with a ball hog.

Meanwhile, the receiving team, on the other side of the net, must cope with all these stratagems and tactics. What kind of formation should *they* take?

Historically, the movement has again been toward the net. For first serves, the receiver typically stands a foot or so inside the base line, on an imaginary diagonal drawn from the server through a mid-point deep in the service court—in position to cover a serve in either corner. If he thinks he can get away with it, though, he should creep a little closer. It depends on how much speed the server puts on the ball and how well the receiver can handle it. He wants to get as close as he *safely* can, but his first job is to make sure he gets the ball back. For the second serve, he should plant himself a step or two closer because the server can't risk hitting it so hard.

There are four good reasons why the receiver in doubles should meet the ball as early as he can. One, it gives the server less time to reach the net; the return might catch him in no man's land. Two, it brings the receiver himself nearer to the net; he's trying to get there, too, don't forget, and he's the last of the four players who can start in that direction. Three, the sharp kick of the twist, the serve most commonly used in doubles, is minimized if you can take it on the rise, just after it bounces. And four, the farther in the receiver stands for his return, the better cross-court angle he enjoys.

About 85 per cent of returns of service in doubles are hit cross-court at the server rushing in. (We're assuming, for the moment, a conventional serving formation in which the net man isn't poaching.) The receiver's intent is to keep the ball away from the net man and to force the advancing server to make a weak, defensive volley. This first volley in doubles is extremely important. A receiving team that can survive the first three shots—the serve, the return of service, and the other team's first volley—and that can manage to get both partners to the net in that time, is back on equal terms with their opponents. They've dissipated the serving team's advantage.

The trick is in surviving that long. Even among top-flight doubles players, no more than 50 per cent of all returns of service are strong enough to follow to the net. In weekend play, it's no higher than one out of three. The rest of the time, the receiver must stay back, play defensively, and work for an opening.

The most successful return of service stroke is a dink hit just hard enough so that it still has a little "go." It's a safe shot, a relatively slow shot (which gives the receiver more time to follow it in), and if it falls near the net with a very small bounce, the server, racing in, must dig it out and hit up. It's mandatory that a return of service dink be kept low. Ideally, it's hit cross-court over the middle of the net (the net is six inches lower in the center than at the sides), and never bounces higher than the net cord. But it must carry enough speed so that it doesn't just sit there; the ball should play the man at whom it's hit. He should be forced to return it with a low volley or half volley, not allowed to take one step and hit a ground stroke.

Not *all* returns of service, though, should be cross-court dinks. Variety and surprise are essential to winning tennis. Now and then—and especially near the start of the match—you should drive some returns of service straight down the line to discourage the net man from poaching. If he poaches on your dinks, he'll murder you. You should also mix the dinks with lobs and topped drives—drives to which you impart topspin. An offensive lob makes a good return of service when the server is making a headlong rush to the net, moving too fast to stop and change direction, or when his partner's nose is hanging over the net. A defensive lob can help you out of trouble when you're scrambling after a serve hit in the corner. In either case, make sure you give the lob sufficient height. If an opponent at the net can reach it with an overhead . . . well, Tilden, in that position, once smashed a ball so hard it knocked the opposing net man unconscious.

What about unconventional serving formations? They call for special tactics by the receiver. The preferred return of service when the server stays deep—too old or too lazy to follow his serve to the net, or unaware that the one-up-and-one-back system was conclusively proved unworkable in the nineteenth century—is a deep cross-court drive to his feet to *keep* him back there; he won't be very dangerous at the base line. When the serving team uses the Australian formation, returns of service should be aimed down the line; hitting cross-court to the net man is suicide. And whatever the formation, if you catch the net man poaching, hit behind him—a drive down the line or a lob to his backhand. Either will keep him honest in the future. Also, a low shot right at his middle is excellent.

Now let's imagine that the return of service works; it forces the server into a weak, defensive volley. This is where the fourth player, the receiver's partner, takes over. His job is to cash in on opportunity. He intercepts the volley and puts it away—or at least makes an attacking return of it. A good rule to follow in making this shot is "hit your opponent's feet."

The most valuable asset this fourth player can have is the ability to anticipate correctly. Starting from a modified net position—just inside the service line, and a foot or so closer to the center than to the side line—he must constantly keep his mind, his eyes, and his body *ahead* of the tennis ball. He watches the receiver for only a split second—just long enough to learn the direction of the return. (The receiver's position may give it away long before he actually hits the ball.) Then he shifts his interest to the man across the net. Will he intercept the shot? Is he poaching? Is he faking? (All four players, at this critical juncture, are trying simultaneously to confuse the opposition.) He must not make a mistake in "reading" the net man's intentions. Let's say that this time the net man isn't poaching. The server will be making the volley. The fourth man's scan moves swiftly to the server. (All this is happening in a fraction of a second—the fourth man moves his eyes rapidly from receiver to net man to server.) He watches very carefully, sorts out the clues, anticipates the probable direction of the volley, waits until the server is committed to the shot, then moves into position to knock it off. All is usually lost if the opposition has deceived him. But the fourth man is justified in taking big chances; it's one way to bring about a service break in doubles.

Both teams will be confronted with shots hit down the middle that either of the partners could play. To avoid any mix-up, there are certain rules to follow. The first of these is: Communicate clearly. A one-word call will usually suffice—"Mine!" or "Yours!" or "Back!" or "Out!"—something very simple and decisive. Don't ask your partner, "Can you take it or should I?" If he's in the better position to decide, keep quiet and let *him* do the calling.

The player in the left court, with his forehand toward the center, should usually hit a ball that comes directly down the middle. There are two possible exceptions to this rule, however. The first is when a return of service is hit down the middle. The net man, regardless of whether he's playing the left court or the right, should move over and attempt to intercept it. The other exception is in a point-blank exchange. The partner who made the last shot should take returns hit down the middle. He usually finds it easier to follow the ball and to anticipate the way it will come back.

On cross-court shots, the partner more distant from the hitter—the one on the opposite side of the court—should usually make the return. Incidentally, when both players can reach an opponent's cross-court shot, it does *not* necessarily mean they're playing too close together. "Packing the center" or "crowding the middle" provides extra coverage to the low part of the net, where most shots are directed in doubles.

Chapter 5

THE GENTEEL BATTLE OF THE SEXES:
MIXED DOUBLES

LAST SUMMER I heard about a man from Manhattan who drove up to Connecticut for a weekend of casual tennis and found himself scheduled for a mixed doubles match against a woman he didn't know. Imagine his feelings when she arrived for the event in a filled out maternity dress. Concerned that she might have her child on the forecourt, he was exceedingly careful all through the match not to hit too hard in her direction. Consequently, he gave her a good many setups, which she managed to put away for easy winners—enough of them so that her side won the match. After it was over, she unbuckled her belt and pulled out a big, fluffy pillow. The pregnancy had all been a ruse.

That's the sort of thing that can go on in mixed doubles—a lot of fun, a lot of psyching, a lot of men driven nuts.

Like many young players who take the sport seriously, I avoided mixed doubles for a number of years. It seemed to me a frivolous debasement of "pure" tennis, and I took it up only as an expedient. I was entered in a tournament in Seabright, New Jersey, where it was the policy in those days to feed and house the players only as long as they remained in competition. As soon as you were eliminated, there went your meal ticket. Since mixed doubles was the final event on the program, I signed up for it to get the extra days of free room and board. I was astonished by the discovery that I *enjoyed* playing mixed. It was fun and, besides that, you met a lot of girls. There are always pretty girls around tennis courts—have you noticed?—and many of them are looking for partners or opponents. All you have to do, when you see one you like, is ask her if she wants to hit a few. Usually the answer is yes. Going around the circuit playing more and more mixed doubles with a succession of incredibly lovely partners, I sometimes wondered how other athletes— football players, say—struck up an acquaintance with a girl. Does a defensive guard sidle up suavely to a blonde and say, "How about you and me finding a field somewhere, baby, and tackling each other awhile?"

Anyhow, I liked mixed, and played enough to get good at it, and eventually I teamed up with Margaret Osborne. We were well on our way to winning the fifth national championship when we were sidetracked by a typically bizarre mixed doubles incident. We'd gotten to the finals and had set point in the first set when I pedaled back to cover a lob. Don't ask me why—it's still a mystery to this day—but I lost it and it landed on my head. The Forest Hills crowd roared with laughter. Flustered and embarrassed, I was thrown off my stride and we lost both the set and the match.

And don't think that's the *worst* thing that's happened to me in mixed. I was even more humiliated in Adelaide, Australia, when I was teamed with Nell Hopman against Colin Long and Nancy Bolton in another mixed doubles final. The tournament was one I wanted badly to win. My record that season in Australia had been frustrating: no championship trophies at all. But I was determined to go home with at least *one* piece of hardware, and this looked like the perfect opportunity. After a strongly contested, two-hour struggle, Nell and I had finally reached match point on my service. "You can't blow it now," I kept telling myself as I took my position at the base line to serve. I concentrated hard on what I intended to do: get the first serve in, hit it deep to Colin's backhand, and follow it very quickly to the net. (Rule 1: Get to the net. Remember?) I tossed the ball up, hit it, and made a headlong dash forward. In the next couple seconds I formulated rule 1A: Get to the net *standing up*. Crossing the service line, my feet flew from under me and I slid across the forecourt and right under the net, like Maury Wills stealing second. Lying there helplessly, flat on my back, I watched Long's return land untouched in my court. Again my team went on to lose the match.

In "mixed troubles"—as tennis players call it, often with good justification—you have to expect what that nickname suggests. Play hard, try to win, but don't take it as seriously as you would if the other sex weren't involved. Keep your sense of humor and enjoy yourself.

The tactics are the same as for regular doubles, but with modifications to give the man a heavier work load. Now don't misunderstand. I'm not suggesting for a second that the woman be assigned a subservient role. I'm not one of these male supremacists on the court. I don't go along with Tilden, for example, when he says that the gal should position herself "wherever she would be least in the way." The only time I remember playing doubles with that attitude, my partner was a male, a show-biz male, an atrocious tennis player. He said it was more important to him to win than have fun—it's possible he'd made a slight wager on the outcome—and he asked me how that best could be achieved. I could see he was serious, so I gave him a straight answer. "As soon as the ball is in play," I told him, "just run full speed off the court." The strategy worked well enough that we won the match—or I won, however you'd like to phrase it.

But the point of mixed doubles is for everyone to have fun, and the gal has no fun when the man hogs all the action. On the other hand, sharing things 50–50 is impractical; accommodation should be made in the typical mixed doubles partnership for the man's longer reach and bigger stride. I think of it as approximately three feet down the middle. When I'm playing mixed, I mentally move the center line over about a yard in my partner's direction. With the alleys, a tennis court is thirty-six feet wide. If I cover twenty-one of this thirty-six feet, my partner is left with fifteen. That's a seven-to-five ratio or, translated into percentages, about 58 per cent to 42 per cent. I'm convinced that for a typical mixed doubles team, that's a reasonable division of labor. Again, though, I perhaps should point out that Tilden differs. "Once in a while," he says, "you find a girl who really gets into the game and plays her one third of the match, which is all any sane man would allow her to play." But girls are better players now than they were in Tilden's time. And so, for that matter, are men.

A side-by-side formation is preferable in mixed, just as it is in regular doubles, but one-up-and-one-back is often necessary and permissible. Usually it's the lady who elects to stay back. Either she can't volley or she's openly afraid. "Play at the net?" she says. "*Me?* Don't be silly. The ball moves too *fast* up there." I've known girls who never got within twenty feet of the net until the match ended and they came up to shake hands.

I have to point out, though, that both partners will soon be exhausted using the man-up-and-girl-back formation—the girl because she'll be covering the entire backcourt by herself, not just the twenty-seven feet used in singles, but also the alleys, which make the court one-third wider; and the man because he'll be frantically busy at the net trying to keep his partner from being run into the ground by intercepting every shot he can get his racket on.

Still, it's probably easier on the male than the reverse up-and-back, in which the *woman* plays the net, providing her partner with what protection she can, which is frequently little or none. If a shot comes right at her, she'll try to return it (assuming that her face isn't covered in fear), but with her small stride and short reach she'll intercept few others. She'll walk off the court as fresh as a daisy and wonder why her partner's tail is dragging. Must be out of condition, she'll think.

So a side-by-side formation is definitely best. If the lady has a weakness, her partner can protect her by indulging in a little more poaching than usual. But again I say: Don't be a court hog. Too much poaching is worse than too little. It can lead to bitter anger, friends screaming at each other, tennis rackets broken over the skulls of guilty partners, even to shattered marriages. Maybe you're familiar with Irwin Shaw's short story, "Mixed Doubles," about a husband-and-wife team playing an emotionally charged match. In the final set, the woman starts thinking about Reno. It should be required reading for every tennis player.

The first rule of poaching is: When in doubt, don't. Never steal a tennis shot away from your partner unless (a) you can hit it from a much better angle, or (b) hit it sooner, when the other team is vulnerable, and (c) you have a good chance—at least two-to-one—of putting it away for a winner. The poach should be regarded as a knockout punch. You want it to end the point. Otherwise, you'll have pulled yourself out of position and given the opposition a big opening to hit for.

I'm speaking now, of course, about the offensive poach, the attacking poach, the so-called poach of opportunity. You see a chance for a quick knockout and you go for it. The defensive poach is a different matter entirely. Here, you see your partner is out of position, so you move into his territory to play a ball he can't reach. Rather than accusing you of stealing his shot, he'll thank you for saving the day. And that's what you'll be doing: just trying to keep alive. You're in no position to go for an outright winner. That's not the intention of a defensive poach. You're scrambling, holding the fort until your partner can recover. It's a good time to throw up a high defensive lob.

The best position for any two partners to play is where their weaknesses are least exposed. Often the gal's backhand is the team's Achilles' heel. In that case, they might use the Australian formation. This is a reverse alignment, as we saw in the last chapter, in which the serving pattern incorporates a poach. The partners stand in tandem on the same side of the center line rather than at the usual diagonal. Many mixed doubles teams employ this formation, especially when the woman is serving from the left court, to protect her against a cross-court return of service to her backhand.

In the first few matches you play with a partner, you'll discover what weaknesses he or she has. It's a little like courtship and early marriage—a man and a woman bound in a delicate relationship that can either blossom happily or quickly turn sour. It pays to be tactful, conceal your disappointments, and be considerate of the other person's feelings. I always tell both parties not to bicker or complain—to be stingy with their criticism but free with their praise. Talk it up, be cheerful, and boost your partner's morale.

Beyond that, my advice for men is different than for women. So at this point, let's segregate the class according to sex for the purpose of separate counseling—ladies first, as chivalry demands.

Talbert's Ten Time-Tested Pointers For Women

◄ Always let your partner appear to be boss. You know he isn't, and I know he isn't, but in the interest of maintaining good team morale, indulge him in this innocent delusion. Few things more effectively destroy a man's ego than to have a woman give him orders on the tennis court. Not that it doesn't happen—and quite often. I recently saw a man about six foot four teamed with a gal who was barely five feet. I'll say this for her: What she lacked in physical size, she more than made up for in shrewishness. Don't ask me why the guy took it; I can't imagine. *Suggest*, if you must, ladies, but give in on disagreements. I'm probably typical of men who play tennis in that my favorite partners are those who comply sweetly with all I say.

◄ Pay attention to what you're doing on the court. Shall I tell you why so many men are reluctant to play mixed doubles? Because so many women (not you, of course, but probably some of your friends) allow their minds to wander. Halfway through the match, they're a thousand miles away. Never again, the man solemnly vows. Ladies, I implore you from the bottom of my heart on behalf of male tennis players all the world over: *Please* try to concentrate completely on the game. It's the only way to win or to be a popular teammate. Your partner will forgive you for your frequent poor shots. He'll shrug off your many violations of sound tactics. He'll pretend to be amused when you lose track of the score. He'll overlook your abysmal ignorance of the rules. All these other failings he expects and will accept. Men who play tennis are by nature very tolerant. The only thing he will *not* feel obliged to put up with is your refusal to concentrate. That's the one unforgivable sin.

◄ Even if you're a much stronger player than your partner, pamper his ego by allowing him to serve first. And let him play the left court when receiving. By denying him these two prerogatives you'll be questioning his masculinity.

◄ Never start to gossip with your female opponent—or with anyone else, either player or bystander. Girls who turn their matches into long-winded gab fests are enough to make a man give up tennis for golf. Talk only to your partner, talk only about tennis, and always keep your comments brief.

◄ Don't take the attitude of a junior partner or underestimate the importance of your role on the court. It pains me to say so, but the record bears it out: The woman in mixed doubles is more important than the man in determining which team wins. (Tell your self-important partner to put *that* in his pipe and smoke it.) This is just as true at the highest levels of the game as in competitive weekend play. Since the enemy normally concentrates its attack on the woman—in keeping with the so-called weak-link theory—victory hinges on which gal is better. Her partner, assuming he's reasonably competent, is more or less along for the ride. Take me. I'm a living illustration of the point. After I teamed up with Margaret Osborne to win the national mixed doubles titles, and was consequently feeling pretty proud of myself, she punctured my ego by going on to win five *more*, with three different men as her partners—Ken McGregor, Ken Rosewall, and Neale Fraser. As far as the tournaments were concerned those boys were just Tom, Dick, and Harry. The titles were won by Margaret.

◀ For heaven's sake, don't wear jewelry on the court. The constant jingle-jangle of necklaces and bracelets will drive your partner crazy. (Of course, if he has wronged you and you're trying to get even, you've stumbled on the perfect device.)

◀ By all means, show up the other man if you can. Women are often better players than men, and the rules permit rubbing it in. Pass him with a backhand and shout, "The weaker sex? Ha!" Jerk him around with a blistering drive and yell, "Equal opportunity for women—now!" Nail him with an overhead in no man's land and cry, "Death to the double standard!" The audience will love it and so will your partner. And psychiatrists recommend it as good therapy, I'm told. Working off your aggressions, they call it.

◀ Don't make effusive apologies for your errors. Your partner knows you didn't give the point away on purpose. You don't have to offer him assurances. Learn whatever lesson your mistake should have taught you and then put it out of your mind. Concentrate on winning the next one.

◀ When asking a man you haven't played with before to serve as your partner in a mixed doubles match—which is acceptable etiquette on the tennis court—make sure he knows your drawbacks as a player. Diabetics sometimes wear a little metal tag around their neck that says, I AM A DIABETIC. IN CASE YOU FIND ME . . . blah, blah, blah. Maybe girl tennis players should wear something on that order, right out where everyone can see it. MY BACKHAND IS LOUSY, the metal disc might say, or, I REFUSE TO PLAY UP AT THE NET. Before he gets stuck with a partner like that, a man has a right to know it. And never take advantage of your good looks or friendship to ask a man who plays out of your class to be your partner. He'll be torn between the misery of playing beneath his level, which is torture to a serious tennis player, and the risk of hurting your feelings by declining. Actually, it's usually wiser not to ask the man outright, but simply to let him know that you're available to be his partner, and then let him do the asking, if he wants to.

◄ Play to win. After all, that's why you're out there.

TALBERT'S TEN TIPS FOR MEN

◄ Always ask your partner if she'd like to serve first, but only as a courtesy—she's expected to decline—never as a serious suggestion. So rarely does the woman serve first in mixed doubles that I can remember being a party to it just once. And that time my partner asked *me* the question. She walked onto the court and said, "Would you like me to serve first?" Flabbergasted, I could think of nothing else but to yield. This was in Chicago, a charity match, and our opponents were both national champions—Vic Seixas and Maureen Connolly. My partner played brilliantly and we won, 6-2, 6-3. But she was scarcely a weak-link pitty-pat player of the type found so frequently playing weekend mixed doubles. She could hit with more authority than a good many men. Her name was Althea Gibson.

◄ On the other team's service, stand firmly in the left court and *then* ask your partner which side she'd like to play. It's a question like Althea's; it permits of just one answer. But form in these matters is considered important. You'll be flattering your partner by implying that you think she's good enough to play either side, while simultaneously relieving her of the necessity of choice. The truth is that few women can play the left court even passably well, and it's foolish to let them try. Direct her to the right side, where she belongs.

◄ Don't pick on the opposing lady *unless you have to*. Concentrating your attack on the gal spoils her fun. Besides, it's more satisfying to show up the man. On the other hand, when you're desperately in need of a point, Tilden's advice still holds. "The whole theory of winning at mixed doubles," he said, "is rather unfair and definitely ungallant. It is that the first time the man gets the ball he should hit at the other woman as hard and in as difficult a position as possible." I'd add one refinement to that piece of advice. After you've slammed the ball past her for a winner, apologize profusely that you meant to hit it elsewhere.

◄ When serving to the lady, use a pronounced slice or American twist. It *looks* a lot softer than a faster delivery, but without being easier to return.

◄ Never issue blunt commands to your partner. Always put your orders in the form of suggestions. "Do you think it might help if we lobbed more often?" This flatters her into thinking her opinion counts and avoids unnecessary friction.

◄ Don't insist that your partner play net if she's reluctant. Encourage her to, but don't force it. Unless she can volley, she'll feel uncomfortable there and your chances of winning will be diminished.

◄ If you spare the other lady by not hitting to her weaknesses, don't let your own partner know about it. Such are the workings of the female psyche that she'll consider it a form of betrayal.

◄ Choose your partner on the basis of her skill, not her beauty—especially if your wife or girl friend is present. Nonplaying women tend to be touchy about these things.

◄ If your partner mistakenly calls an opponent's shot out, discreetly hold your tongue. It's better, just this once, to ignore the code of ethics and turn a deaf ear to the other team's protests (eventually, they're bound to get over it) than to correct her and incur her displeasure. She'll never forgive you if you contradict her on a call.

◄ Give it your best. Women like winners.

Chapter 6

THE SUBTLE ART OF PSYCHING

THE COMPILERS of Webster's New World Dictionary apparently included no tennis players; they left out the verb "to psych." Omitting "racket" or "ball" would make just as much sense. The importance of psyching in the game of lawn tennis has been evident ever since 1874, when the first two players walked onto a court—one of them feigning an injured ankle, no doubt, and the other shouting brashly to a friend across the way to stick around and watch him win in straight sets. Nor has it gone out of fashion since then. There's an element of psyching in every weekend tournament and every international match. In 1969, in Mexico City, in the Davis Cup matches when Mexico beat Australia—thus preventing the Aussies from getting to the Challenge Round—Rafael Osuna, the Mexican star, who shortly afterward was killed in an airplane crash, accused the Australian captain, Harry Hopman, of deliberately causing disturbances to annoy him. The third set of the deciding match, the New York *Times* reported, "was marred by noisy demonstrations by the unruly crowd of 5000." Hopman's fierce arguments with the umpire and linesmen did little to calm things down. "Hopman knows that when I get mad I can't play well," Osuna said, "and that's the only reason he did all that out on the court. It's just psychological warfare." But somehow—perhaps partly because of the high altitude of Mexico

City, which the Australians were unaccustomed to—Osuna and his teammates won anyhow.

The purpose of psyching, or psychological warfare, is to fluster your opponent and undermine his game. Within the limits of the code of good sportsmanship, which the following chapter takes up in more detail, you can do it any way you can think of. The more original, the better. Upset his confidence. Jar his composure. Play on his sympathy. Spoil his concentration. Turn him inside out and leave him screaming.

As any veteran player can attest to from experience, the assortment of ploys is unlimited. One afternoon down in Texas, for example, Gardnar Mulloy and I, who were then national champions—this was in 1949—were playing in a tournament against two unranked youngsters who were having a hot day; everything they tried was hitting chalk, it seemed. In the third set they'd gotten a service break on us and were one game from winning the match. Our plight was becoming desperate. Mulloy decided to do something about it during the change of sides. He walked over to whichever of our opponents was to serve the next game, threw his arm around him, and complimented him extravagantly on his play. "You know, Talbert and I aren't exactly slouches ourselves," he said. "We've won the Davis Cup doubles, four national championships at Forest Hills, just about every big tournament you could name. Maybe you're not aware of it, but it's been almost nine years now since we lost to an American team. If you kids manage to end that string today, the whole world will know you tomorrow. Every sports page in the country will carry your picture. I'd just like to say, son, that I wish you good luck. Fame is only four points away." Then he beamed that big-brotherly smile of his and walked very slowly to position—to give the kid a lot of time to think it over. You could finish the story yourself, I imagine. The youngster was so nervous when he started to serve that he could barely toss the ball in the air. From that point on, we blew them off the court.

That's one useful tactic: give the enemy the jitters. Another is to get him—or her—angry. The ladies are particularly adept at this technique. One walks up to her opponent before the match and says, "Why, Janet, your outfit looks absolutely stunning! I didn't *know* they made tennis dresses in size sixteen." The victim needs three or four games to recover.

Distracting the other guy's attention works, too, but the gimmick of planting trim blondes on the side lines has perhaps been overdone. Try to be a bit more imaginative. A player named Earl Cochell once pulled a beauty on me. I was beating him pretty handily on a hot afternoon when he asked for permission to go back to the clubhouse and change his long pants for shorts. The pair he was wearing when he returned to the court instantly caught my eye. As he very well knew, I admire attractive clothes. But it wasn't just the fact that these shorts were good-looking; something else about them drew my notice. I couldn't figure out what it was, though. It bothered me through the rest of the match. Afterward, when I told him I admired those new shorts, he laughed and said, "That figures. They're yours." *That's* what it was! Of *course* they were mine. I'd bought them the previous day. This rascal had cunningly plucked them from my locker and used them to psych me with. If I'd lost, I'd have broken his neck.

Thousands of incidents like these, Mr. Webster, might justify amending future editions of your dictionary to accommodate the word *psych* (sīk), *v.t.* [from psychology].

An occasional variation—call it definition two—could properly be labeled the self-psych. In this one, the player isn't spooked by his opponent; he manages the job all by himself. You've probably seen a few self-psychers on the court. They're easily recognized. Usually, their most distinguishing characteristic is that they make their best shots in practice—or during a game after play has been stopped. Visualize anxious Andy, for instance. (Let's call him Andy instead of "Player A," as a reminder that all players are human, not robots, and are subject to human frailties.) Picture Andy in position to receive a hard serve. His opponent is the local Gonzales. The ball ticks the top of the net coming over—not enough to change its flight in any noticeable way, but nonetheless a let has been called. Andy relaxes, and with a free and easy motion he smoothly hits the ball back to the server—a return that Rod Laver might envy. Okay, now Pancho winds up and fires once more. This shot is the first serve all over again but just high enough so that it misses the net. The ball remains in play. Andy is suddenly all tangled up; his swing is awkward and tentative; his return goes into the net. Why did he hit it so differently this time? Because this time, you see, it counted. The pattern is that of the classic self-psycher—the player who betrays whatever skill he possesses by always tensing up in competition.

Experienced players have a nickname for Andy. They call him Oki Choki, the Japanese tennis professional—referring to his tendency to "choke" under pressure. He "gets the steelies," as they say, or "gets the elbow" or "gets the lump." For obvious reasons, few chokers win trophies, but now and then you'll spot one on the national scene, if only for a brief time. A few years back, there was a promising young player who, in a match against Dick Savitt, then ranked second in the country, broke Savitt's serve in the last set. The chance to pull an upset played havoc with his nerves, though, and he blew the match with four straight double faults. Savitt just stood there looking on in amazement. For all he contributed to his opponent's collapse he could as easily have been in the clubhouse showering.

But you can't count on playing Oki Chokis very often. Normally, if you want your opponent psyched out, you'll have to engineer the job yourself. Either you can utilize the long-term psych, which erodes his nerves through relentless gnawing at them—some players, for example, don't consider it indecent to call, "A little long!" when an opponent's shot falls beyond the base line, or, "A little wide!" if he hits it outside the court, insidiously emphasizing his every mistake—or you can try a sudden psych that surprises him. Better yet is to blend the two in subtle combination, the way a boxer might punctuate a body attack with quick, stinging blows to the head. Many weekend players, it might hearten you to know, are the equal of the top stars as psych artists. Maybe you can't hope to have a serve like Clark Graebner's, but if your mind is sufficiently fertile and devilish you might surpass him as a student of the con game.

Whether you could top Harry Hopman, though, is doubtful. Hopman, long the captain of Australia's Davis Cup team—which played in the Challenge Round for thirty straight years before that string was broken in 1969—is a genius at psychological warfare. One year when the stalwarts of our own Davis Cup squad were Tony Trabert, then ranked first among American players, and Vic Seixas, rated immediately behind him in the standings, we were greeted in Australia by a story on the sports page that showed Hopman was already at work. He had said in an interview that our rankings were cockeyed because Seixas was the better of the two—clearly an attempt to sow the seeds of petty jealousy and distract the Yanks' attention from winning. It was the opening salvo in a long campaign of psyching that would last until the matches were over.

One lesson to be learned from Hopman's success is that psyching always calls for proper timing. Invariably, there's a very best moment to attack—the absolute instant when the victim is most vulnerable to whatever kind of fun-and-games awaits him. Once when I was scheduled for a match against Frank Sedgman on a grass court made slippery by a sudden brief rainfall, I discovered I'd forgotten my spikes. The only other player there whose feet were my size was Sedgman's Australian teammate, Mervyn Rose. I explained my plight to Rose, who handed me his own spikes and told me I was welcome to use them. Hopman was informed but said nothing. Before long, I'd completely forgotten about the spikes and was concentrating hard on beating Sedgman. That assignment was always formidable, but not, I thought, impossible. I figured I could do it if I just kept bearing down and refused to let myself become distracted. Then, all of a sudden, here comes Rose onto the court, yelling, "You'll have to take the spikes off, Billy!" Right smack in the middle of the warm-up, this was—no more than two minutes before the match was to start. "Hopman says I can't let you have them," Rose explained. Then it dawned on me, painfully, what I'd let myself in for: another shrewd Hopman psych job. Naturally, my shattered concentration lay in ruins by the time I'd put my sneakers back on.

Fortunately, I can report to my fellow Americans that we once got back at Hopman for his tricks—in 1954. That was the year we brought the Davis Cup back home on the strength of beating the Aussies at doubles. We split the singles matches, 2–2. And partly why we beat them at doubles, I'm convinced, was the back-to-the-net signals system we sprung on them. Signals had been used sparingly up to that time and were usually of the simplest sort; the net man would indicate his intentions to his partner by hand signs or, more often, word of mouth. As captain, I decided to use a slightly different method, a way-out system that Mulloy and I had experimented with a dozen or so years before. The net man would face his serving partner, turning his back to his opponents, and give the signals like a catcher in baseball. It was just a fancier way to do the same old thing, but the Australians got all shook up. It caught them by surprise and made them mumble. What were these crazy Americans up to? Why were they turning around? The answer was simple: to rattle them. And apparently it worked—at least we won.

Don't infer from all this talk about psyching, however, that a winner needs no other talent. He must always have the game to back it up with. Otherwise, it's just a big, boring bluff. Actually, the best players are automatically good psychers, even if they spend no effort on it. They psych you by consistently winning. Bobby Riggs used to have that effect on a lot of us. He still does, as a matter of fact. We play against each other every now and again, and I notice that he still has the knack. Bobby blends the reflexes of a superior athlete with the analytical mind of a first-class chess player and the instincts of a riverboat gambler. That's a tough combination to contend with, take my word. At one point in history, my record against Riggs stood at thirty-two losses, no wins. Talk about being demoralized. He can psych you just by picking up a racket. And the thing about Riggs is that he not only beats you but teases you to death in the bargain—all those little tantalizing junk shots. He'll lure you a half step too close to the net, then kill you with a lob shot *barely* out of reach that gently plops behind you on the base line. When he sees the puff of chalk, he'll maybe scowl in mock disgust. "Don't tell me that actually hit the *line*," he might say. "Boy, I can't seem to do *any*thing right. I meant it to be in by six inches." Lovely. Drives you straight up the fence. (Believe it or not, though, I eventually beat him. Later in the book I'll tell you how.)

So far, I've mentioned only negative psyching, the kind designed to give a guy the willies. There's another type, too, with just the opposite intent—the anti-psyching psych, you might call it. Its purpose is to strengthen the morale or the performance of a teammate, doubles partner, or friend. Too many players ignore it.

In December of 1968, when Don Dell was the captain of the U. S. Davis Cup squad, he presented each player with a big team picture, inscribed: "You paid the price—we won. Thanks. Donald." He handed them out on December 25, which was the day *before* the Challenge Round began. That's what I mean by a positive psych—a gesture that inspires strong confidence.

In weekend tennis, kind words can help immensely. Good-natured ribbing is always lots of fun, but try to mix it up with honest praise. Most now-and-then players are starved for encouragement, and what's wrong with giving them some? They might return the favor one day. Mind you, I'm not suggesting that you praise them unduly. If someone plays tennis like Smokey the Bear, don't tell him he reminds you of Tony Roche. He won't benefit from being lied to. But usually there's at least *one* aspect of his game that merits a legitimate compliment. Maybe his overhead smash is pretty good. When he scores with it, give him some support: "Great shot, Henry! You really powdered that one!" It helps relieve the pain of his disasters.

Even the best players often need this kind of handling. In my years as the captain of the United States Davis Cup team, one of my biggest jobs was building confidence. I remember occasions when our number one player fretted night and day about how lousy he thought he was. Building up his confidence for a critical match was a full-time job in itself. The first thing we'd do when we arrived in a foreign country was to seek out a good local chess player; chess was the only thing we ever discovered that could keep this guy from worrying about his tennis. After that, I'd sometimes have a talk with Dinny Pails. Dinny was a superior player in his own right who worked out against our boys to keep them sharp—a combination coach and sparring partner. I never asked Dinny to ease up against this boy—that would defeat the whole purpose of the practice session—but maybe I'd tell him to imagine that the side lines were six inches closer to the center, say. Then at least he wouldn't nail the fellow with shots that sprayed chalk and, by doing so, deflate his morale. It goes without saying that when the young man hit a good one, Dinny was effusive in his praise.

I'd better not tell you this second player's name either, but he's the principal in what I think of as my $50,000 psych. For convenience, let's just call him Charlie. Once again, our lacking in talent Davis Cup team was visiting Australia, and Charlie got a bad case of nerves. Among the symptoms was an inability to get to sleep nights. First he changed hotel rooms four or five times, then he tried sleeping on the floor. It didn't work. "Cap, it's this city. I can't sleep here," he told me. He wanted my permission to stay in the suburbs, in the apartment of a girl he'd met.

"Oh, come on, now," I told him. "If the press ever found out . . ."

"No, no. It's nothing like that," he said. "No sex. I just want to sleep." Searching desperately for a player, I reluctantly gave him permission.

Three or four days later, when he *still* couldn't sleep, he decided it was his rackets; he needed new ones. So we put in a transpacific call to California and ordered another batch flown out at once. That ploy didn't work either. Neither did bending the training rules to allow him a glass of port now and then.

By this time, I was genuinely concerned about the boy, and I brought in a doctor to examine him. His conclusion was that Charlie was on the verge of a nervous breakdown. He recommended that I withdraw him from the interzone finals we were scheduled to play that week against Belgium. I mentioned this to Charlie when we were sitting in a restaurant and he was holding a glass of beer. (Beer was something else we'd tried in an attempt to calm his down.) The news so distressed him that he crushed it in his hand—literally squeezed the glass so hard it shattered. "*Please*, Cap," he pleaded. "You've *got* to let me play. Anyhow, who do you have that can replace me?"

His point was well taken. I really had no one. Charlie was one of the best players on the squad, and we needed him to win against Belgium. It was the last step in reaching the Challenge Round, and $50,000 was at stake. That was how much had been invested in our trip, and we wouldn't get it back unless we qualified for the Challenge Round and a share of the gate receipts. I finally sought the counsel of a second physician. This one wrote a prescription for some little red pills—tranquilizers—that he assured me would get Charlie through the match. So I decided to let him play, and during the match at crucial junctures I gave him another red pill.

Unfortunately, the match was a long one—five sets—and in the last set I ran out of pills. On the next change of sides, with the games 5–4 in his favor, Charlie was preparing to serve for the match. "Hurry, Cap!" he said. "Give me another of those pills. I'm not going to make it without one."

"Okay, just open your mouth," I said. "I'll toss it down your throat." He did, and I popped in a salt tablet. He then went out and put a happy ending on the story by winning the match that advanced us to the Challenge Round.

A player uncertain of his skill with a racket is always susceptible to psyching on the court. Your only sure defense is to play the game so expertly that you're confident that no one can beat you. Beyond that, you can guard against enemy psyching through anticipation and concentration. Don't let the other guy catch you off guard, and no matter what happens, stay cool. I first learned the lesson the hard way from Martin Buxby, a nationally ranked player in the '30s. Buxby was aware that I played my best tennis when a brisk, steady rhythm prevailed; I liked to find a groove and stay in it. From this he deduced, with impeccable logic, that needless interruptions would annoy me. When we met in the Southern Championships, I settled in a groove and was wearing him down when he delayed the match during the change of sides by requesting some orange juice from the clubhouse. Perhaps because Buxby was one of the top-seeded players, the umpire went along with the request. The incident made me furious. The rules quite specifically prohibit such tactics; play is to be continuous. What Buxby had pulled—and of course I couldn't blame him (anything to fluster an opponent who's winning)—was like a prize fighter, glassy-eyed and sagging to the canvas, getting the referee to call an intermission. It so irked me that I blew my lead and lost. The next time we met—it was several years later, at Forest Hills in the national championships—I anticipated something similar, and sure enough, he tried it again. This time his gimmick was to send the ball boy to the clubhouse to exchange his tennis shoes for spikes. I had to admire him for keeping a straight face; the court was about as wet as Death Valley. But somehow he again won the umpire's approval. Maybe it was the same guy, I don't know. My reaction on this occasion, though, was simply to smile. And I concentrated even harder, while Buxby was waiting, on how I intended to atone for the last time. When play resumed, I beat him good and proper. Walking off the court, he commented wryly that the spikes hadn't done him much good. "You should have stuck to orange juice," I said.

Psyching can often be deflected. Recently in trying to psych someone else, I got my comeuppance. Peter Bostwick, World's Court Tennis Champion, and I entered the Southampton Invitation Doubles Tournament. We did it as a lark knowing that we would probably be zapped in the first round. But it turned out that there was another team who had entered for laughs: Dick Squires, leading platform tennis expert and Herman Schaefer, financial vice-president for Pepsico. As luck (and the officials) would have it Squires and Schaefer were our first round opponents. The center court was dusted off for this battle of the titans. As we walked over to it, I got in my psych.

"Last time I was on this court," I remarked, "I beat Gonzalez."

Schaefer came right back.

"Who is that?" he said. "Irving Gonzalez?"

Much of the satisfaction of psyching your opponent is in dreaming up original ploys. But there are many standard tactics that work well, too, and I offer you some as a way to get started:

◄ Pick up your opponent's racket on the side lines and say, "Do you always have it strung with this much tension?" The strings can be either loose or tight. You're just planting a doubt in his mind.

◄ In the warm-up, say, "Boy, aren't the balls hard these days? They're getting tougher all the time to control." Then just see if his control doesn't falter.

◄ If it's hot, wear your sweater a little longer than usual to show him that the heat doesn't bother you.

◄ When he blows an easy overhead, say, "Maybe it's this altitude. A lot of players say it gives them trouble." Again, it doesn't matter if you're in the Alps or at sea level—all you want to do is start him thinking.

◄ If the wind's strong and he's using a heavy racket, say, "I always thought a light racket was better in the wind. How come you're using a heavy one? If he *is* using a light one, just reverse the words "light" and "heavy."

◄ Maybe he's wearing wool socks with nothing underneath them. Say, "I always heard you were supposed to wear cotton under wool. That way, the wool doesn't mat."

◄ Examine his shoes and say, "We're playing on asphalt. Why are you wearing clay court soles?" Or vice versa. If his shoes look somewhat scruffy, make him conscious of the fact: "I always whiten my shoes after a match—just like Don Budge did."

◄ And of course you must arrive with more rackets than your opponent. If he carries two, you should manage to have three. If he shows up with three, you top him with four—even if you have to borrow all but one.

Positive self-psyching is another knack you should acquire. In some players, it seems to be nothing more than superstition. Art Larsen, for example, got the nickname of "Tappy" by tapping his racket on the ground before each point a specific num-

ber of times; some days it might be four taps, other days six—
maybe it depended on his horoscope. In any case, he thought
it helped him win. Tony Roche, the young Australian, has a
thing about tennis shorts; he refuses to own more than one
pair, his "lucky" pair. Last year, during a tournament at Madi-
son Square Garden, Tony's "lucky" tennis shorts were stolen
from his locker and he called me on the telephone in panic. I
rushed him a new pair, and he played as well as ever, but the
incident didn't break him of the habit. Now it's *those* shorts he
considers to be "lucky."

Even if he relies on self-deception to get it, a tennis player
needs a positive outlook. He must think in terms of winning,
not of losing. A defeatist frame of mind must be avoided. Some
people find this a difficult task, but even Vic Seixas finally
learned. I remember him being interviewed by a newspaper reporter just before a Davis Cup match against Ken Rosewall.
The two of them had met on eight previous occasions, and Rosewall had won every time. The reporter asked Vic what his
chances were this time. Seixas gave the question considerable
thought, then answered that the odds were very strongly in his
favor because no player had ever beaten him nine straight times.
Now that's what I call taking a positive view of discouraging
circumstances.

Chapter 7

THE UNWRITTEN CODE

ON THE ASSUMPTION, occasionally justified, that tennis players are ethical, intelligent people, formal rules have been kept to a minimum; it's left to the discretion of the players themselves to resolve many touchy situations. Although flattering, this arrangement can easily lead to trouble if a player doesn't know about the unwritten code—rules of good sportsmanship, etiquette, and manners—or if he conveniently decides to ignore it. Let me illustrate with some typical examples.

Imagine a close match in which General Gamal Nasser, representing the United Arab Republic, is paired against Moshe Dayan, of Israel. (Why not? Isn't tennis an international game? Don't people of many different interests enjoy it?) The circumstances dictate that they play without officials, since neither will accept any neutral observer whose name has been suggested by the other. Okay, so they'll call their own shots. Early on, General Nasser lands a ball near the base line that may or may not have been in; Dayan is honestly not sure. He hesitates a second, then opts for magnanimity and gives his opponent the point. A little while later, it happens in reverse; a ball lands very close to Nasser's base line—too close to make a positive call. Nasser suggests they call a let and play it over. He then wins the replay, which happens to be match point. Observers predict no improvement whatsoever in Arab-Israeli relations.

◀ RULE ONE: Turn about is fair play. Don't accept a dubious judgment at one point, and then, later on, in similar circumstances, deny it to your opponent.

Consider another international match. Raquel Welch of the United States is playing Brigitte Bardot of France. (I have no idea whether either plays tennis, but it would be a hell of a match to watch.) Both are at net when Brigitte throws up a lob. Neither girl sees where it lands. The court is surrounded by spectators, all males, and Raquel undulates over to one and asks him where it hit. He assures her it was out by six feet. Meanwhile, Brigitte has inquired of someone else, who comforts her by saying it was in by a yard. Ultimately they locate an honest observer who replies that with both young ladies at the net, no man whose eyesight was unimpaired would have been looking at a ball in the backcourt.

◀ RULE TWO: Keep spectators out of it. They usually feel obliged to give you *some* kind of answer, but it's often either uninformed or biased.

A different source of trouble is the indecisive player. Have you met this type on the tennis court yet? Ask him if he has difficulty making up his mind and his answer is, "Well, yes and no." He can tempt you to break a racket over his head. Let's say you serve him a cannonball near the line—maybe it's in, maybe out. He attempts to hit it back but at the same time yells frantically, "I don't know if it was good! I'm not sure!" What kind of a call is *that?*

◀ RULE THREE: When in doubt, shut your mouth and keep playing. Don't share your uncertainty with others.

Then there's the guy—we can call him the Judge—who deliberates every verdict. He refuses to arrive at an ultimate decision until every piece of evidence is in. In the middle of an extended rally, for example, a wayward ball might come rolling across the court. Rather than instantly stopping play by calling "Let!" the Judge waits patiently for further developments. Ten seconds later, after losing the point, he sagely concludes that, yes, the loose ball was distracting and it would be only fair to play the point over.

◀ RULE FOUR: Make "let" calls without any delay, or forever hold your peace. The same thing goes for "out" calls. There are delayed calls in hockey under certain circumstances, but in tennis second chances are frowned on.

Here's one that possibly you'll question my word on, but I assure you it can happen and it does. Connie and Irene play grimly for two hours without exchanging so much as a word. At the end of the match, someone asks them who won. "I did," says Connie, "6–3, 6–2." Irene answers differently: "I did—6–4, 6–1." Well, at least they agree on the number of games. And perhaps they've discovered the ideal scoring system, the one that makes *both* players winners. Unfortunately, the narrow traditions of tennis discourage this type of variety.

◀ RULE FIVE: When necessary to avoid discrepancies, have the server give the score before each point.

One of our better-known American players once had a lesson in behavior imposed on him in a national juniors tournament. He got angry at himself for missing an easy setup and slammed the ball over the fence. The umpire, to his credit, calmly stopped play and offered the young man two choices: retrieve the ball or forfeit the match. He retrieved it and soon developed better manners.

◀ RULE SIX: Keep your temper in check. Football players kick their helmets in frustration, and golfers have been known to wrap clubs around a tree, but tennis players should exert more self-control. Petulance and ill manners have become much, much too common, especially among younger Americans. The list of bad actors in this country is a long one. Australia, on the other hand, has almost none. Maybe juniors tournaments should be preceded by a briefing at which the players are informed that vile language and bad conduct will immediately put them out of competition. There *are* other ways to express your frustration. Gardnar Larned, a former national intercollegiate champion, was two sets ahead of Budge Patty one day, then managed to let the match slip away. This was at a tournament in Culver, Indiana. He calmly tucked his six rackets under his arm, carried them to the end of a hundred-yard pier, and walked off it into Lake Maxinkuckee, clothes and all.

Every player's composure is often tested, of course. Occasionally it approaches the breaking point. Here's a situation that's always hard to take. You serve a wicked twist serve deep to your opponent, who barely manages to get his racket on it. His return is a frail little dying-swam effort that you easily put away with an overhead. But your serve was so perfect—precisely in the corner—that your opponent hopefully thought it was out, and so called it. He yelled, "Out!" while in the process of attempting the return, which was largely a reflex action. Further investigation shows the ball was *not* out; it was probably your best serve in a month. So what do you do? Claim the point? Throw a tantrum? No, a let is called and you play the point over. Obviously, if the other guy had missed the serve completely, the point would be given to you; likewise if he had hit it into the net or out of bounds. But since he kept it in play—no matter how feebly—a let is the accepted procedure. Granted, his mistake has deprived you of a point you probably deserved to win. But what if you'd missed that overhead? Would you have given him the point then, regardless of his "out" call? Would you still feel like a victim of injustice?

◄ RULE SEVEN: Give your opponent the benefit of the doubt— not only by calling close shots in his favor but by assuming his mistakes to be honest. And don't do it grudgingly. Be a good sport about it. He'll feel bad enough because of missing the call.

◄ RULE EIGHT: A call of "out" or "let" stops play.

Of course, there are limits to what your opponent should get away with. You are *not* required to tolerate an attempt to have a let called on the ground that he didn't see your placement, for example. It was good by three feet, but he wants to take it over because he was facing in the opposite direction. Maybe he argues that it's each player's duty to call all the shots on his side of the net, and how can he call a ball he didn't see? The best answer is perhaps another question: What's to prevent you from playing blindfolded all day as a means of never losing any points?

◄ RULE NINE: You're obliged to assume a point is good unless you see it land out of bounds. (If the ball *does* go out, though, and the other player sees it, he naturally must tell you so. The intent is never to trick an opponent but to arrive at a fair decision.)

The disc jockey syndrome is one often seen in doubles. One or both members of a partnership sustain themselves with interminable chatter. Post mortems are conducted after every point; mutual encouragement is constant and loud, clearly audible five courts away; all aspects of the game are talked to death. It reminds you of what Frank Lloyd Wright had in mind when he remarked that turning on a radio any more is like lifting the lid off a sewer.

◄ RULE TEN: Keep all conversation on the tennis court brief, especially when the other team is preparing to hit—it constitutes an unfair distraction. Actually, you shouldn't need to talk much any time. Doubles partners can communicate with short, simple calls. "Yours," "Mine," or "Out" is all it takes.

Can you conceive of out-and-out cheating in tennis—that genteel lawn game for people of good breeding? Well, I hesitate to stick any pins in your illusions, but occasionally it happens, even at the poshest clubs. Sometimes a player becomes so intent on winning that his eyesight is adversely affected; he calls "Out!" when his opponent's close shots are cleanly in. The rules hold little recourse for the victim of such robbery except when officials are used. Disputing an opponent's call is poor form, so about all you can do is suffer in silence or simply discontinue the game—and in either case, not play the guy again. A third possibility is for interested bystanders to intervene on the victim's behalf. I remember one occasion in Newport, Rhode Island, when a young man from Yale was playing Bob Falkenburg, who later was to become the Wimbledon champion. In the absence of any linesmen, the Yalie was claiming points that were blatantly not his. A group of us happened to be wandering by—Jack Kramer, Gar Mulloy, myself, a couple others —and saw instantly what was happening. We decided to enlist in the cause of justice by appointing ourselves as officials. Mulloy walked over without a word of explanation and planted himself at the base line. Kramer took the service line, and the rest of us, in turn, assumed other appropriate positions. The match ran its course without incident. Not one word of accusation was uttered, but the obvious implications of our silent rebuke had a lasting effect on the youngster. Since that day, he has been a generous and considerate opponent, one of the game's most popular players.

◄ RULE ELEVEN: Play fair or risk ostracism. Tennis players don't like cheaters.

A curious exception to the foregoing rule is the current attitude concerning foot faults. Many players, including the best ones are inclined to take foot-faulting lightly—*too* lightly, in my estimation. A foot fault consists of stepping on or over the base line before you deliver your serve. At least half of all weekend players, probably more, are consistently guilty of it—sometimes by only a couple inches, sometimes by as much as two feet. The distance doesn't matter; all foot faults are illegal. I urge you to consider them as such. Don't shrug them off because "it's only a weekend tournament." That's unfair to the players who heed them. I mean, look: if you want to play tennis, play the rules. The rules in this regard are specific. A foot fault is a handicap unilaterally arrived at. I'll say it more bluntly: it's cheating.

◀ RULE TWELVE: Never foot-fault.

A comment often heard wherever tennis players gather is, "Show me a good loser and I'll show you a loser." Generally speaking, the statement is valid; everyone should always want to win. But sometimes you *will* lose, and the way you accept it goes a long way toward determining how other players judge you. If you offer the winner a limp-fish handshake, or sulk, or make excuses, or tell him he was lucky—such behavior won't enhance your popularity. Even worse is to quit trying in the middle of a match when you're getting your brains beaten out—"going into the tank," as tennis players describe it, or they might say that you've "got your Jantzen on."

◀ RULE THIRTEEN: Lose like a tiger, then accept it like a man. Your opponent deserves the satisfaction of feeling that he beat you fair and square.

◀ RULE FOURTEEN: Be gracious when you win too. Don't rub it in with some condescending comment or with a gesture that makes the loser feel worse. Do *not*, for example, yell loudly across the court as your defeated opponent troops wearily away, "Hey, Harvey! Want to hit some? I really need a workout." The opposite tactic of making your opponent feel good is highly recommended—regardless of which of you won. Gottfried von Cramm, the former German star, was fiercely competitive while a match was in doubt, but a model of cordiality afterward. We once played each other for the German singles championship at the Rot-Weiss club in Berlin. When the match was over, he met me at the net, smiled, shook hands, and generously commented, "I haven't faced ground strokes like that since Don Budge. It was a genuine pleasure to play you." The scoreboard indicated that

I was the winner, but I assure you that as far as I was concerned, von Cramm was a winner too.

That's fourteen points for you to keep in mind while playing. Woodrow Wilson needed only that number to outline his plan for world-wide peace, so fourteen should suffice for the more limited purpose of maintaining harmony on the tennis court. But perhaps I might add an extra word or two here on the subject of gamesmanship.

To some people, gamesmanship is synonymous with psyching, but I think of them as being slightly different. I think of gamesmanship as a more inclusive term. Psyching is only one aspect of it. Psyching is entirely psychological in nature—that's where it gets its name. Gamesmanship, on the other hand, can be physical as well. Let me illustrate what I mean with an example. Once in a tournament in Rumson, New Jersey, at the Seabright Lawn Tennis and Cricket Club, I was scheduled for a match against Sidney Wood. It was an afternoon match, and on the morning of that day, Sidney invited me to go swimming. I was only an innocent kid from Cincinnati, and the surf was a novelty to me. I plunged in and had a good time. It wasn't until after the match was over and Sidney had beat me by a lopsided score—6–1, 6–1, I believe it was—that I realized how neatly he'd conned me. He hadn't so much as gotten his knees wet that morning. He just sat on the sand cooling his feet in the water, conserving his energy for the forthcoming match, and cheering me on as I sapped all my strength paddling around in the surf. This embarrassing incident was gamesmanship but not psyching. Psyching is when you get a man to thinking too much. At Seabright, I wasn't thinking at all.

Wood deserves high marks for his gamesmanship that day, but you'll notice that it occurred off the court. On-court gamesmanship is a drag. Most players, including me, have little tolerance for it. Maybe under special circumstances—the fifth set of a Davis Cup rubber match, for instance—it might be reluctantly condoned. But usually it's simply a bother. It's like the golfer who scrutinizes every blade of grass before he attempts a putt. If his name is Jack Nicklaus and he's one stroke off the lead in a tournament where first price is $30,000, let him study the green all day. But weekenders who do likewise with nothing at stake are just stalling and annoying other players.

The ploys on the tennis court that constitute gamesmanship could probably be numbered in the hundreds. A player stops every five minutes to tie his shoe again. Or he questions the linesman on every call. Or he claims the net is too high—or too low. Or he keeps asking to have the score repeated. Changing courts, he'll deliberately pick up the wrong racket and realize it only when the other guy starts serving—then back he strolls to get the right one. Or he insists on using his "lucky" ball and won't serve with any of the others he's given. If he wears glasses, he probably keeps taking them off, ostensibly for the purpose of cleaning them but actually just to bug his opponent. Or he tosses the ball up then catches it without serving, just to throw the other guy off stride. Or he pretends he's not ready when his opponent starts to serve—either that or waves his racket to distract him. Or he "accidentally" kicks the ball—an obvious stalling tactic. You could think of variations without limit.

To my way of thinking, these are simply bush tactics, petty and unwarranted annoyances. They remind me of the story about Moses and Saint Peter and the day they went out to play tennis against each other. Moses' first serve was deep to the backhand, and Saint Peter wasn't able to handle it. He hit it way out of the court. It would have landed at least twenty feet beyond the base line except that a miniature whirlwind blew up and prevented the ball from falling. Then an eagle swooped down, clamped his beak around the thing, and carried it back toward the court. Just above the base line, a bolt of lightning struck his tail and shocked him into releasing the ball; it dropped right on top of the chalk. Moses just glared at Saint Peter in disgust. "All right," he said, "did you come to play tennis or are you just going to clown around?"

Chapter 8

DO YOU REALLY KNOW YOUR TENNIS?

To BE THE WINNER in a tennis match, the best-of-five sets, you must score at least how many points? Seventy-two, correct—four points in each of six games in three sets. So let's make that the passing grade for this short quiz on tennis, designed to test your knowledge of the rules and procedures. There are twenty-five questions. Give each of them four points. If you get at least eighteen right, you're a winner.

1. A receiver standing behind the base line is hit in the leg by a serve before it touches the ground. Is a fault called, a let, or does someone win the point?

◀ The server wins the point unless the ball ticked the net going over, in which case a let would be called. The rules say such a serve is officially in play until it actually touches the ground out of bounds, and any player who touches a ball in play automatically loses the point.

2. What if the server tosses the ball up, swings at it, and misses?

◀ First of all, he'll probably feel humiliated. On top of that, he's charged with a fault. But if he catches the ball or lets it drop without swinging at it, no fault can be assessed—though nothing in the rules prevents his opponent from snarling and accusing him of gamesmanship. Another possibility is that the server, in tossing the ball up, accidentally releases one or two others from his hand and stands there in a shower of tennis balls. The rules say a let should be called, not a fault, assuming he didn't swing. The embarrassment is penalty enough.

3.   Can you return a ball before it passes over the net—just reach over and hit it back while it's still on your opponent's side?

◄ Not legally. The only time your racket is allowed to pass over the net is after you've hit the ball—in other words, as part of your follow-through. There exists, however, one exception to this rule. You *are* permitted to hit the ball on your opponent's side of the net if it has already landed on your side first and then been carried back over to his side again by either a strong wind or sharp backspin. In that single instance, you can reach over and hit it. If you *don't* hit it, in fact, your opponent wins the point. But as always you must avoid coming in contact with the net. Should your body, your clothes, or your racket brush against it, you've lost the point right there.

4.   During a doubles match, can the members of one team switch positions so that the player who was receiving in the right court takes the left court instead?

◄ During a match, yes; during a set, no. The same rule applies to serving. Whatever order the partners decide on at the start of the set must be maintained throughout that set but can be changed for the next set, if they wish. Incidentally, the order of serving and receiving may be different; the partner who serves the first game is not required to play the right court and receive first.

5.   Does the receiver have to stand in any specific area of the court?

◄ He doesn't have to stand in the court at all if he'd rather post himself out of bounds. All that's required of him is that he stay on his side of the net.

6.   With the score at deuce, the server gets ready to deliver

into the left court and then realizes that he got mixed up somewhere along the line and should actually be serving into the right court instead. No one knows how many points have been served from the wrong half. What should be done about it?

◄ The mistake should be corrected by having the server move over to the proper court at once, but the score remains unchanged. Any point completed before an error is discovered is always permitted to stand. The same goes for service faults. If the server had delivered one fault from the left side before discovering his error, he would make his second delivery from the right side with one fault already chalked up against him. Sometimes in a doubles match, one partner will inadvertently serve two games in succession. If the error is discovered before the second game is finished, his partner should serve the rest of that game according to the original pattern. But if the error goes undetected until *after* the second game, the serving order for the remainder of that set is reversed. In other words, the overlooked partner serves the next game. Otherwise, one player would serve three times in succession.

7. Is the receiver permitted to volley a serve—that is, hit it back before it touches the ground?

◄ No. To do so costs him the point.

8. When are the players supposed to change sides?

◄ After each odd-numbered game of each set. In a nontournament match, sometimes every three games works better —though every two games is what it says in the rules. As in football, simple chance decides which player starts where. A racket is spun or a coin tossed. The winner of the call may elect to serve or receive in the first game, *or* he may choose one side of the net. The loser gets whichever choice is left. The position of the sun or the direction of the wind often makes the choice of sides important.

9. A tournament match is interrupted by a rain storm with

the games 2–1 in the first set and the score in the fourth game 40–30. From what point does play resume the next day?

◀ From exactly where it left off. Tennis has no equivalent of the rule in baseball that requires the completion of four-and-a-half innings before anything counts. Play picks up in tennis as if there had been no interruptions—same score and same serving and receiving orders.

10. When a ball is obviously heading out of bounds, should you stop it or let it go by?

◀ Touching it in a tournament will cost you the point. The rules say a ball is considered to be in play until it actually hits the ground out of bounds. But in tournaments there are ball boys to do your retrieving. In weekend play, you'll save a lot of time and energy by agreeing to amend this one rule. If a ball is quite obviously going out of bounds, common sense suggests that you stop it. The critical word here is "obviously." In fairness to your opponent, you should let it go by if there's any doubt at all in your mind—or if there might be any doubt in *his* mind.

11. In a doubles match, the receiver seems ready for the serve but his partner is out of position. Should the ball be put into play?

◀ No. The server should wait if either of his opponents is unready. To do otherwise constitutes a "quick serve," which is very bad manners. Technically, however, a quick serve in these circumstances could rightly be blamed on the receiver rather than the server, for the receiver is obligated not to indicate his readiness until his partner is also set. An unmistakable signal for the server not to fire yet is simply to hold up your hand.

12. When are new balls brought into play?

◀ Whenever you agree on before the match gets under way. In major tournaments, it's typically after the seventh game, then every nine games for the duration of the match. If you want to, you can think of it as every nine games, with the warm-up period counting for two games. The reason for the odd number is that it alternates the advantage of serving with fresh balls, which are harder to return; a ball on which the fuzz is still tight tends to sail. In some tournaments a much used practice is to open a new can of balls at the beginning of every set. But that might be expensive or unnecessary; a can of balls can often last two sets or more.

13. After delivering one fault, a server makes the second one good only to have his opponent call a let because a player from an adjoining court runs into him while attempting a difficult save. Obviously, the server will have to serve over. Does he do so with one fault against him?

◄ No. Once a server has successfully put the ball into play—whether on the first try or the second doesn't matter—a let gives him two brand new chances. Of course, when the service itself is a let—when the ball ticks the net before landing in the proper court—it is not deemed to have been put into play. In other words, if the server already has one fault against him, a let serve does not annul that first fault.

14. How many rest breaks are permitted during a match, and when?

◄ The rules say that play shall be continuous with the exception of one ten-minute break, which for men and juniors (males in the eighteen-year-old class) comes after the third set. This rest period follows the second set, however, if the players are women, seniors of either sex, or boys or girls under sixteen. Notice that the change of sides is not accompanied by a rest break; a maximum of one minute is allowed.

15. What happens if a player is injured or exhausted? Is play stopped to allow him to recover?

◄ "Play shall never be suspended, delayed, or interfered with for the purpose of enabling a player to recover his strength or his wind." So reads one excerpt from the official rules of tennis. When a physical affliction keeps a player from continuing, he loses the match by default. The single possible exception is a temporary disability caused by an obvious accident; the umpire, at his discretion, may call time in such a case. But this must *never* be done for simple fatigue or for any affliction—cramps, for example—brought on by a natural loss of physical condition. Weekenders, however, might modify this rule in the interests of reasonableness.

16.   In doubles, the server's delivery glances off his partner's racket and caroms over the net into the proper court. What's the ruling?

◄ A fault. Any serve that hits the server's partner, his clothes, or his racket is judged a fault no matter where it ultimately lands.

17.   What if a ball in play hits another one lying on the court?

◄ Play continues unless it's impossible to tell which ball is which. In that case, a let should be called.

18.   Who should make the call on a close serve in a doubles match played without officials?

◄ Generally, the receiver's partner, since he has a good view of the service line and the half court line and isn't concentrating on returning the ball. If the serve lands close to the side line, however, the receiver himself may be in a better position to call it. Occasionally, one player will call a ball out of bounds and his partner will call it good. In that case, a reasonable doubt is assumed and should be decided in the other team's favor. This applies not only to the serve but to any shot.

19.   Is using two hands on the racket permitted?

◄ Permitted, yes, but not recommended. Don't be swayed by the knowledge that a few top-ranked players—Pancho

Segura and John Bromwich, for example—sometimes used two-handed grips.

20. The server delivers a ball that hits the tape at the top of the net and bounds back toward the middle of the court. Can the receiver request the server to delay the second serve until the first ball has been picked up?

◄ Yes. Any player can ask to have the court cleared at any time, except, of course, when the ball is in play. And he's justified in the action if the loose ball is distracting. But to overdo it is an annoying waste of time. For example, if you're holding two other tennis balls in your hand, there's no excuse for interrupting the action while you walk the whole way up to the net to retrieve a faulted first serve that lies at its base, out of the way. Wait until the point has been decided. After all, that's why you use three balls instead of one—so that play may be continuous. Another considera- tion might be mentioned at this point: In returning a re- trieved ball to your opponent or your partner, don't just hit it casually in his general direction; make an effort to send it to him directly, waist-high, on one bounce. Maybe it seems like a trivial matter, but few things are more irritating on the tennis court than having to retrieve the same ball a second time because the first retriever threw it out of reach.

21. How high is the net supposed to be?

◄ In the middle of the court, it should be exactly three feet (and held taut there by a strap attached to a hook imbedded in the ground). At the posts, which are located three feet outside the court, the net should be six inches higher—precisely three feet six inches. Courts where the net is a uniform height—as high in the middle as it is at the ends—not only violate the official rules of tennis but work against the fundamental tactics of the game, which are pred- icated on the center being lower.

22. In doubles, must the server stand between the center mark and the singles side line, as he would in singles, or may he serve from behind the alley if he wishes?

◄ A server can stand anywhere behind the base line between the center mark and whichever side line is in effect—the near side line if he's playing singles, the far side line in doubles.

23. How can you legally return a ball without hitting it over the net?

◄ By managing to hit it *around* the net—if, for example, you've been drawn far off court by a sharply angled shot. You can even get fancy and bounce it off the net post, at a height either above or below the top of the net, if by doing so you can make it land within the appropriate court.

24. In doubles, what happens to the server who (a) hits his partner in the back with the serve, or (b) hits the receiver's partner in the chest with it?

◄ He (a) incurs his partner's wrath and has a fault called against him, or (b) wins the point because of the receiving team's duty to avoid touching any ball in play.

25. In the process of serving an apparent ace, you lose your grip on your racket and it flies into the net. Do you win the point, is a fault called, or what?

◄ If your racket hits the net while the ball is in play, your opponent is awarded the point. The rules are quite clear on this matter. You lose any point during which your body, your clothes, or your racket touches the net, the posts, or the ground within your opponent's court. And in this case, the ball would not be considered out of play just because it had passed the receiver. Theoretically, he can return it until it bounces again. If your racket hits the net before that second bounce, tough luck. Of course, if your racket misses hitting the net, if it lands on the ground on your side or out of bounds, the serve is considered an ace. The penalty is not for losing your grip but for hitting the net with your racket. Deliberately *throwing* your racket, however—if you hit the ball with it—always means the loss of the point.

Chapter 9

GETTING IN SHAPE TO WIN

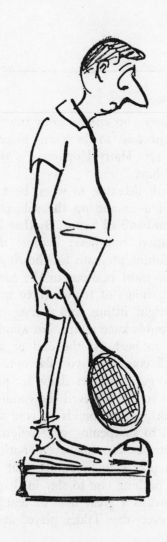

WASN'T IT Napoleon who said an army travels on its stomach?
Well, in a different way, so do tennis players. "Never to get
tired in the gut," says Harry Hopman, "is the greatest asset a
tennis player can have."

Hopman is worth listening to when he talks about fitness.
He's something of a fanatic on the subject. You might call
him the Vince Lombardi of tennis. By that I mean his players
may lose on occasion, but never because they aren't in top
shape. His conditioning program for the Australian Davis Cup
squad is surely the most rigorous in the game. A typical day
might include four hours of tennis, three miles of road work,
a half hour of weight lifting, and a long calisthenics session
with maybe 250 double knee jumps. No wonder the Australians
are always tough to beat. At the end of a grueling, five-set
match, they're still coming at you flat out.

The best way to get in proper shape for playing tennis—and
to stay there once you've achieved the condition—is simply by
playing tennis. Nothing else builds up your stamina so quickly
or is better suited to sharpening your reflexes. Rule one is to
play tennis as often as you can, even if it's just a half hour
at a time. If you play enough tennis, that does it; you'll be
fit. You'll require nothing else to stay in shape. But "enough,"
in this context, means a great deal of tennis. I used to play
six or eight hours every day. Tilden played five sets of singles in

the morning, then another five sets in the afternoon—all of them, he claimed, at full speed. René LaCoste, the former French star, played five sets on the morning of a critical match just as a means of warming up!

For some people, even that much isn't enough to keep in shape. When I was the captain of the U. S. Davis Cup team, both of our top stars, Vic Seixas and Tony Trabert, played a great deal of tennis every day. It sufficed to keep Seixas physically trim, no matter what he ate or how much. But poor Tony, despite those long hours on the court, still had to compensate with twenty-five pushups for every bite of candy he took.

There are other ways, besides playing tennis itself, to get yourself in shape for the game. Following a reasonable diet is obvious, as are the other basic rules of sound health. Sports such as handball and squash are very good; like tennis, they take stamina and quick reflexes. Jogging, so popular in America today, is a big help in improving your wind and leg muscles. (For a tennis player, the stomach muscles are first in importance, then the leg muscles, then the muscles of the arm that wields the racket.) Isometrics and aerobics, if you don't become bored with them, can also help keep you fit. More interesting perhaps are these wild modern dances, and you don't even have to have a partner; just stand up and throw yourself around the room awhile.

There are lots of ways to exercise in the course of the day without putting much demand on your time. Walk instead of driving short distances, for instance. If you regularly travel by subway or bus, make a habit of getting off it a couple stops early and legging it the rest of the way. Climb the stairs instead of taking the elevator up if it's no more than three or four flights. A practice I often urge on my businessmen friends is to keep a tennis ball around the office. Then when you get nervous and want something in your hand, it doesn't have to be a cigarette. Pick up the tennis ball and repeatedly squeeze it for whatever length of time you'd spend smoking. That way, instead of cutting your wind with tobacco, you'll be building up your wrist and arm muscles. Tobacco and tennis make a poor combination. I'm no expert on the other risks smoking involves, but I've seen a lot of tennis players panting on the side lines as the consequence of a pack-a-day habit. I've certainly never regretted not smoking.

Frank Parker had a way of keeping fit you might try. Do you remember the name Frank Parker from the '40s? I do, and for excellent reasons. Twice he defeated me in the finals at Forest Hills for the U.S. singles championship. Parker kept fit with what he called "shadow tennis." There's no reason you couldn't play it in your back yard or on your driveway, although Parker usually used a tennis court. He went out there with a racket but no ball and no opponent. Someone, often his wife, would stand at the net and call out make-believe shots. "Return of cross-court forehand," Mrs. Parker might say. Frank would then visualize the shot in his mind and dash over to make the return. Then, "Backhand down the middle," and he'd turn heel and chase it. For a half hour or so, she'd keep him running, changing pace, giving him a genuine workout. It's good exercise and also good practice. So is playing a regular game of tennis without a racket. You catch the ball and throw it back, which means you have to move farther because you can't reach out and hit it with your racket. Incidentally, if your opponent uses a racket you should win; it's easier to control a ball throwing it than hitting it.

Practice can be as good exercise as an actual game, but too few players like to do it any more. The young ones coming up have no patience. It's particularly true of Americans, sad to say, that they're unwilling to spend more than a minimum of time perfecting their shots in practice. Hitting against a backboard seems a relic of the past. For the great old-time

players, it was a regular routine—a hundred cross-court forehands, a hundred down the line, followed by an equivalent
number of backhands, all hit against a wall over a net-high
stripe of paint. That's what they attributed their victories to:
constant and intelligent practice. And in practice, you should
always get to the ball on first bounce; don't just stand there
and await its arrival.

Not all practice is intelligent practice of course. Some of it
is just lackadaisical fooling around, a self-indulgent waste of
time. Weekenders who need a lot of work on their backhands
run around the ball and hit forehands instead. What good is
practice like that? But I'm not speaking only about weekenders
here. The attitude goes right to the top. At the moment,
Arthur Ashe is rated first in this country. Recently I watched
him work out against Dick Savitt. It was a perfect opportunity
for Ashe to practice ground strokes, which happens to be the
weakest part of his game. Savitt hits the ball about as well
off the ground as any tennis player we have. Yet Ashe spent
the whole time pampering his instinct to rush to the net and
volley. He benefited very little from the session. And it isn't
as if Arthur had perfected his game. He still has a long way
to go yet. For a player with such an abundance of natural skill,
he shouldn't lose as often as he does.

So actually playing tennis is one way to stay in shape, and
practicing the game is another. But what if you lack the
facilities or the time? What if it's winter and you're stuck in
the city without access to a court or fancy equipment? How
can you keep fit for next summer?

Okay, I'll outline an exercise program, but look: I don't
want you to be a heart attack victim. If you're out of condition,
or over forty, or have a weight problem, or if you've recently
been under a doctor's care, check with him before you begin.
And in any case, start slowly and work up to a full effort.
The first thing to exercise is good judgment.

I'll confine it to fifteen minutes a day, and the only equipment you'll need is a jump rope. It makes little difference what time of day you exercise. For some people, the best time is just before bed; for others, the first thing in the morning. Or you can make it after work or at noon if you like—just so it's the same time every day.

And don't plunge right in; take time to loosen up. In exercising, as in actual competition, it's a mistake to overexert yourself too soon. Devote a few minutes at the start of each session to just getting the kinks out of your muscles. Start off with something like running in place. Reach down and touch your toes a few times. Then try a dozen jumping jacks. Do you know that old army exercise? From a standing position, you jump in the air, spreading your feet about shoulder-width apart and at the same time swinging your arms up in an arc until your hands meet over your head; then jump again and return to the starting position. When you're tired of doing jumping jacks, lie on your back, kick your legs up, and peddle a bicycle—thirty seconds ought to be enough. Then stand back up again, put your hands on your hips, and twist your torso to the left just as far as it will go, then as far as it will go to the right. By the time you've completed ten twists in each direction, you should be warmed up enough to begin.

I've told you how important strong stomach muscles are, so let's start by doing some sit-ups. They're excellent for strengthening your abdomen. A sit-up is the same thing as touching your toes except that you're lying down instead of standing. You therefore have to work against gravity. Lie flat on your back and have someone hold your feet down—or you can hook them under a heavy piece of furniture. In any case, your heels should be flat on the ground so you don't slide all over the place. Next, stretch your arms straight over your head. Then just sit up, touching your toes, and lie down again. Establish a steady rhythm and keep your knees straight.

At first, you'll probably manage about thirty in one minute —up on the first count, back on the second. Later, you should double that pace: *one*-and, *two*-and, *three*-and . . . like that. When you're able to do sixty in sixty seconds, you can level off and just do that much each day.

For the second stomach exercise, I'll offer you a choice. I'll list three and you can pick any one of them. In each case, you begin by lying flat on your back, your arms extended on either side, your feet lifted slightly off the ground.

In the first—call it "draw bridge"—you slowly raise your legs, keeping them together with knees unbent, until they're straight up, perpendicular to the ground. Then, just as slowly, lower them again until they're almost touching the floor but not quite; to let them touch would defeat the whole purpose. Try to keep them elevated as long as you can, constantly changing the angle. The position you'll find most difficult to hold—with your feet just barely off the ground—does your abdominal muscles the most good. Get so you can hold it at least a full minute.

Let's call the second choice "going around in circles." The starting position is the same as for draw bridge, but you rotate your legs instead of raising and lowering them. Slowly start circling both legs to the left, trying to make a larger circle with each revolution, then stop and, without letting your feet touch the ground, do the same thing in the opposite direction. The bigger you make the circles, the better.

"Scissors" is an appropriate name for the third choice. You begin with your feet lifted slightly off the ground again, but this time you raise your upper body as well, and prop yourself with your elbows and hands. Then what you do is to crisscross your legs like the blades of a pair of scissors. Alternate which leg is on top. Do it fast, and for as long as you can.

The best way I know of for strengthening your leg muscles is by doing squat jumps for one minute each day. It will seem like the longest sixty seconds of your life, the first time you attempt it. A squat jump is exactly what the name implies. With one foot slightly in front of the other, squat down low, almost sitting on your heels. Then jump as high as possible, put the other foot in front, and return to the squatting position. Repeat it again and again without stopping. Eventually, you should manage about one every second—sixty during your one-minute sentence.

Then, for your arms, get down and so some pushups. Everybody knows how important it is for a baseball pitcher to keep his arm in shape. Well, the same thing goes for tennis players. A baseball pitcher in a typical game will throw the ball a hundred times or so. In a five-set tennis match, you'll serve about that often, maybe more if you commit a lot of faults. Add in all the other shots, and you'll make about a thousand swings a match. So it's very important that your racket arm be strong. The other arm doesn't really matter very much, but unless you can manage to do one-arm pushups, you'll have trouble trying to exercise them independently. Remember that the more pushups you do every day, the harder it will be for an opponent to beat you in the late, crucial stages of a match. You're undoubtedly familiar with the way to do pushups. Lie on your stomach with your hands beneath your shoulders, then push yourself up until your elbows lock, keeping your back rigid, your legs straight, knees off the ground. Then lower yourself until either your chin or chest touches, then right back up again. A man in good condition should be able to do fifty. Women can be excused after a much smaller number if they don't want bulging shoulders. In fact, I'll even excuse them from pushups entirely if they simulate a comparable number of serves, either with or without a racket.

Last on the program are the agility exercises—first off, skipping rope. Start slowly with the regular two-step skip, do it for a dozen times that way, then hop-jump on one foot, hop-jump on the other, again for a dozen times on each, then return to the two-step and pick up the pace. Your goal is to skip at maximum speed, just as fast as you can swing the rope, for five minutes uninterrupted.

To wrap up the session, you can pick one of three: the star jump, the jackknife, or the double knee jump. Each one begins in the standing position.

For the star jump, you simply leap as high as you can and fling out your arms and legs. At the peak, you should look like a four-pointed star, or like an "X," if you want to think of it that way.

The jackknife is a modified air-borne split. When you leap, you throw your legs apart as high as you can get them, ideally as high as your waist. Then touch your toes with your hands. Lots of luck.

The double knee jump, alias "the kangaroo," is easier for most people to accomplish, but not much. Learning the proper balance takes time. You leap into the air and, at the peak of your jump, raise both knees until they touch your chest. This is *not* the same thing as just bending your knees and kicking yourself in the rear. *Lift* your knees and touch them to your chest. The kangaroo is the exercise the Australians are so fond of, the one they might do 250 times without stopping. If you reach one-fifth that number, you can quit. It's been a profitable fifteen minutes.

Some people wonder whether swimming is effective as a means of staying fit for playing tennis. Frankly, there are better ways to do it. As an all-around conditioner, swimming is fine; it improves your wind and maintains muscle tone. Certainly it's better than no exercise at all. But its usefulness to tennis players is limited by two factors. First, the two sports use different sets of muscles; those most important to you out on the court aren't specifically strengthened by swimming. And second, in contrast to the quickness of tennis, your movements through the water are slow motion; swimming does nothing at all for your timing except possibly to take the edge off it. Tennis players who say Ping-pong is a better conditioner aren't being funny at all. I could name any number of world-class players—Fred Perry, Chuck McKinley, and Bobby Riggs, for example—who spent hour after hour playing table tennis. It helped them sharpen their reflexes. Especially on the morning of a critical match, it's a better idea than going swimming. I told you how Sidney Wood defeated me at Seabright after conning me into a dip in the ocean.

Swimming isn't the only thing to avoid before a match. Overeating is another common error. I don't mean to suggest that you starve yourself; that would only undermine your stamina. Just don't load up on rich or heavily seasoned foods a few minutes before you take the court. Eat a sensible, nourishing, well-balanced meal that ends at least an hour before you play.

Younger players seldom have much trouble with food, but they frequently go overboard on soft drinks. And the hotter it is, the more they consume. They gulp the stuff down by the gallon, it seems—before, during, and after their matches. The practice is one no trainer would condone. Indulging in cold drinks on a hot day while you're exercising is a blueprint for getting sick.

Playing tennis, you should not consume a great amount of liquid. A few sips of water while changing sides is all right, or maybe a glass of orange juice or Gatorade, which adds glucose to your system while quenching your thirst, but never any carbonated drink or one with ice. (You might also take a salt pill while changing sides in hot weather, to minimize the risk of stomach cramps. Cramps are a common occurrence in tennis—arm cramps, leg cramps, stomach cramps, you name it. I've often seen players double up on the court with stomach cramps so strong they couldn't walk for twenty minutes. Naturally, they lost the match by default. "Tired in the gut," as Harry Hopman would say.) As for liquids after the match, before you take your shower you can indulge in a small amount —but still not anything iced. Some players like fruit juice. Others drink plain water. My personal preference is hot tea with lemon. Later, when I've showered and have clean, dry clothes on, I'm ready for something iced. How much of it depends on who's buying. And I always hope I'm buying, of course; the drinks are on the winner in tennis.

If you're playing a court that lacks facilities for showering, always put a sweater on after the match and walk around awhile to cool off. Just to sit there in damp clothes invites sore muscles. You should also wear your sweater during the warm-up period, and during the first few games in cool weather. It reduces the danger of "tennis elbow," a painful, throbbing stiffness in the joint, more accurately known as tendonitis. It isn't restricted to tennis players; many other athletes get it too. Johnny Unitas, the Baltimore Colts quarterback, had a bad case of "tennis elbow" not long ago that made him wince every time he threw a pass. I know how he felt. I've experienced it myself. One time, I couldn't lift my hand above my waist, the pain was so intense. I'd crammed too much tennis into too brief a time. The customary treatment is with heat packs or massage or, ultimately, cortisone shots. Believe me, there are better things to have. I urge you to do everything you can to avoid it by following the same rules that baseball pitchers do: Keep your arm warm, loosen up slowly each time out, and be especially careful early in the season. Don't rush onto the court the first warm day and start swinging with all your might after a six-month layoff.

I've known a few players who trained *too* conscientiously. Always in bed by ten o'clock, nothing any stronger than root beer to drink—they turned it into a self-imposed martyrdom. They never had any fun. And why play tennis if you aren't having fun? Others have allowed tennis to become an obsession that eventually betrayed them. I particularly remember Pancho Segura in 1945. He was possibly the best player in America at that time and was determined to win the nationals at Forest Hills. His preparations for the championships knew no limit. He had a pro with him, analyzing his tennis game at breakfast, lunch, and dinner. If Pancho didn't dream about his cross-court forehand, I'd be very much surprised. Well, it was simply too much. He was hopelessly over-tennised, and I beat him for the first time in my life.

That reminds me of my promise a couple chapters back to tell you how I finally beat Riggs. My record against him on the morning it happened was no wins and thirty-two losses. This was in Asheville, North Carolina, where you see all those beautiful southern belles, and the night before the match I was invited to a party that I intended to leave by ten or ten-thirty in order to get plenty of sleep. But I was having so much fun there and my chances seemed so poor ("You in training for your thirty-third loss?" someone asked me), that I allowed myself to be persuaded to stay on—first until midnight, then one o'clock, then two . . . well, you get the picture. I arrived at the clubhouse for the match in my dinner clothes, never having been to sleep at all. In the car driving over, my friends from the party had practically hypnotized me by telling me over and over again, "You can beat him, you can beat him, you *know* you can beat him," and as I walked onto the court, lightheaded and loose, that was the only thought my mind had room for. Bobby's usual psyching tricks were completely ineffective. I took him in straight sets, got a standing ovation, and his magic spell over me was broken.

I don't recommend it as a standard procedure, but I did do the same thing one other time successfully. That was in Newport for a match against Ted Shroeder. Again I arrived in evening clothes, again I was loose, and again I pulled an upset. Allison Danzig, of the New York *Times*, who of course didn't know I'd been up the whole night, had an astute explanation for his readers. Shroeder, Danzig figured, was undoubtedly tired; he'd gone swimming before the match.

Chapter 10

THE PLAYER OVER FORTY

NOT LONG AGO Dick Savitt and I played an exhibition match for my younger son's classmates at the Choate school in Connecticut. The umpire, who introduced us from the center of the court, talked about our past accomplishments for what must have been a good five minutes. I guess he figured that the boys were too young to have remembered us, and he wanted to make sure they appreciated who they were seeing. "Mr. Savitt of New York," he announced, "is a former Wimbledon singles champion, former champion of Australia and Canada, former indoors champion of the United States . . ." and on and on through Savitt's long list of achievements. "And Mr. Talbert, of New York," he continued, "is a former American clay court champion, former captain of the United States Davis Cup team, former national doubles champion . . ." At this point a voice floated down from the stands: "*Formerly*, this would have been a hell of a match."

To anyone over forty, the moral is clear: We're none of us the players we formerly were, back there in the halcyon days of our youth, and it's foolish to pretend any differently. In tennis, you can't get away with it. There's always someone younger to remind you of your age—if not with a shouted comment from the stands, then by running rings around you on the court.

Forty is, of course, just a neat, convenient number. Take it as a symbol, not literally. The first signs of aging may appear a lot sooner or they may graciously hold off for a while. Many prominent players have breezed past that milestone with their tennis skills largely intact. Pancho Gonzales, as I write, is forty-two, and even though he doesn't cover the ground he once did, he's still probably one of the top twenty players in the world. In his appearance last summer at Wimbledon, he defeated Charlie Pasarell, sixteen years his junior, in the longest match in the history of that most famous of all tournaments. Gonzales was so utterly exhausted near the end that he was leaning on his racket for support between exchanges, but after five hours and twelve minutes, and 112 games, it was the younger man who finally succumbed, 22–24, 1–6, 16–14, 6–3, 11–9. In the judgment of a number of veteran observers, the match was one of the finest and most courageous ever played: age spotting youth a two-set lead, then ultimately prevailing.

Gardnar Mulloy is another example. At fifty-five, he continues to accumulate victories, sometimes over opponents less than half his own age. I hesitate to guess how many cups and trophies Mulloy has stashed away by now. The first one we won together was in 1942 and he's been hauling them in ever since. But Mulloy is a truly exceptional case. Most of us feel the years a lot sooner.

I stopped playing singles in serious competition at the age of thirty-seven. My quickness and stamina had dwindled a bit, and it seemed logical that I concentrate my efforts on doubles. Oh, I still play singles every now and again, on occasions like that match against Savitt up at Choate, but in a style that's too restrained for world-class play. I still compete in singles at the River Oaks tournament, but last year a reporter wrote that I "ran like a dry creek."

This concession to the fact that one is no longer young can be traumatic for someone who plays singles exclusively until he (or she) simply can't hack it any more. But in my own case I made it without any great pain because I've always had a preference for doubles anyhow. I think it quite likely that you'll be pleasantly surprised if you first take up doubles after forty. By no means is it the slow, "old man's" game you might have imagined. Singles is more physically demanding, to be sure, but not because singles is faster—only because you must cover the entire court by yourself. The pace is actually much quicker in doubles; the ball moves more swiftly back and forth across the net. To win, you need a quick, shrewd intelligence. Singles puts the premium on a young, healthy body. Doubles is more the thinking man's game. You can excel at it for years after singles becomes too demanding. Darlene Hard comes instantly to mind. Darlene has long been one of the country's best players, and in 1969, teamed with Françoise Durr, she won the U.S. women's doubles championship. But in singles she was whipped in the second round.

So my first piece of advice, when the years start creeping up on you, is to begin a transition to doubles. You don't have to quit playing singles abruptly; just gradually taper off. Think of it as progressing to a more complicated game that gives more weight to your experience and wit.

At the same time, you should begin to alter your style of play slightly. Earlier I told you not to take many chances, to play the percentages and wait for the openings. Force the other guy to take the risks that lead to errors, I said; if you settle for simply returning the ball, time will usually work on your behalf. Well, after the age of forty it's different. Time is no longer your ally. You have to take a different approach to the game in the interests of conserving strength. Long rallies mean long matches that are likely to exhaust you and permit a younger opponent to win. So now, you see, you want to keep every point short. At every opportunity—every *reasonable* opportunity—go for the outright winner. You won't be defying the percentages any more because you've been practicing your control for thirty years, let's say. Your odds are much better than they formerly were.

Openings you would have missed by a mile at age twenty you should now be able to hit with consistency.

And when you do hit good placements, it has a psychological value against a younger opponent who is correspondingly lacking in control. He'll be teased into trying the same shots. Surely he can pull them off if an old man like *you* can—that will probably be his reaction. But he won't make due allowance for your thirty years of practice. Young players are inclined to underestimate experience, often to their later regret. He'll accept your tacit challenge, attempt the same shots, and undoubtedly miss four out of five. Taunt him with a couple more well-controlled placements and his game will get wilder and wilder. In race track terminology, you'll win going away.

If this new approach contradicts my previous advice in one sense, it only reinforces another rule of thumb that I tried to impress on you earlier: Eliminate all waste motion. The older you get, the more important this becomes. You *must* conserve your reduced supply of energy. Gonzales stopped agreeing to sign autographs before his matches when he realized that even the small amount of energy it took could be the difference between victory and defeat. Think before you act should be your fundamental rule. There are many ways you can forestall exhaustion. For example:

◄ Never take three steps when two will suffice. If you can get away with it, don't take any steps at all. If your younger opponent wants to retrieve all the balls, by all means let him do it.

◄ Don't lunge picturesquely at balls you can't reach. You can no longer afford the luxury of attempting impossible saves.

◄ Have a definite purpose for everything you do. Direct every action toward winning.

◄ Use only as much backswing as benefits the stroke. Not only will you conserve your energy, but you'll improve your control of the ball.

◄ Avoid an exhausting duplication of effort by getting more of your first serves in. If you formerly settled for 75 per cent, you should raise your sights now to 85.

◄ When an opening presents itself, go for the winner. You can no longer risk dawdling around.

◄ "Dump" a game—or even a whole set—on occasion. Let's say you're playing against a younger opponent, and you wore yourself out in the first set—which you won. You need a little time to recover. The rules prohibit an intermission now, however, so you decide that in the second set you'll coast. You're not simply *giving* it to your opponent, understand. You'd like to see him work hard to earn it. But you expect to lose the set because you're keeping something in reserve, recovering your strength for the third set. If you can play all-out in the third set and win it, you win the match two sets to one. Of course, it's always nicer to win in straight sets, but when older people try it, the match often turns into a route. They simply can't sustain an all-out attack through two consecutive sets. So settle for winning two sets to one when you need that second set to catch your breath in.

◄ Don't pull a self-psych by brooding on your age. Adopt a positive attitude. Think of all those years of experience you can draw on. There's no legitimate reason for you to feel like an underdog just because your opponent is several years younger—though it's often a smart move to *pretend* you feel that way in order to encourage his cockiness. If you psych him into thinking you should never win a point, every point you win will make him edgy. And young, edgy players are among the easiest to beat, even if you're over fifty.

Purely in terms of stamina and speed, you have reason to expect less of yourself when you've passed the age of forty. It's inevitable that you'll slow down and lose a little zip. But your control and consistency should remain as good as ever, and I've been telling you all along that control and consistency are more useful to a tennis player than brute strength. The best players, of course, have both power *and* control, but offered the choice of one or the other, I'd opt for control every time.

The rules we discussed in the previous chapter for protecting your health on the tennis court are particularly pertinent for players over forty. A reasonable diet is mandatory. Moderation should rule the day. Always wear a sweater in the warm-up period, and also during the first few games in cool weather. Loosen up more slowly than you did when you were younger so as not to waste much energy in practice. Avoid excess liquids, wear a sun hat when appropriate, and always put on two pairs of socks. Your tennis clothes, of course, should be comfortable and cool or warm if playing in cool weather. When the contest is over, put your sweater on again and immediately head for the shower. Don't sit around in the shade and get sore muscles.

Slower courts are better than cement for senior players because (a) softer surfaces are easier on the legs and (b) they tend to minimize a young slugger's assets and put a premium on what older players presumably excel at: consistency and control. Also, of course, a slower pace is more suitable for players whose agility has diminished.

Personally, I'd like to see two changes in tennis that would benefit all players, but seniors in particular. First, I'd like to see some pressure taken out of the ball. In my opinion, the ball is too lively at present. The pace of the game is too fast. Reducing the amount of pressure in the ball would slow it down to what I consider a more reasonable speed.

Second, I'd like to see the three-bounce rule adopted. The pros have given it a good trial, and it works. The rule is very simple: The server can't rush to the net until after the ball has bounced at least three times. In effect, this works against the so-called "big" game, in which the server goes immediately to the net. The "big" game is too tough for players over forty, and, in my judgment, not much fun for *any*body.

When playing doubles with a partner who is much younger than you are, it's silly to split the work load fifty-fifty. Don't lose your match because of pride. You'll both have more fun— and a greater chance of winning—if you let him handle something over half. The philosophy is the same one employed in mixed doubles: Let the player with the stronger physical assets cover that much more of the court.

Many senior players switch to a lighter weight racket. A half ounce or so makes a great deal of difference in the course of a thousand strokes. You'd also be wise to use a more relaxed swing as you enter your later years. Ask your wrist to do an increasingly large share of the job. A full, stiff-wristed swing puts great tension on your arm muscles, and tension is extremely exhausting. Remember: Conserve your strength.

I usually put a time limit on my sessions these days, and I recommend that you do likewise. An hour of hard tennis is enough at my age. I hate to see seniors get involved in these matches that go 16–14, 10–12, and so on, and feel obligated to stick it out to the end. Theoretically, such a match could continue forever, and it represents a real threat to their health. Be competitive and try to win, but don't risk a heart attack. Explain to your opponent before you begin that you're limiting yourself to whichever comes first: one hour or two sets of tennis. If you split the sets, flip a coin to see who buys. Obviously, it is also to the senior's advantage to schedule his matches for morning or evening; the glaring midday heat will sap his strength.

Tennis is one of the very few sports that effectively reconcile the generation gap. I don't mean only father-and-son or mother-and-daughter doubles teams, but one-against-one competition. Many a fifty-year-old tennis player can hold his own against someone in his twenties. In most other sports, you'd be risking your life to try it. Baseball, football, basketball, hockey—you'd have no chance whatsoever of winning. And if you can't hope to win, why play? But in tennis, a decrepit old man over forty can atone for a great deal of undeserved abuse the older generation has been submitted to lately. It delights me to see someone like Gonzales or Mulloy teach a youngster some new respect for his elders.

I recently discovered a tactic that minimizes the age gap better than anything else I know of. I tried it in a match with Jean Borotra, the former French star, who must be close to seventy now, about twenty years my senior. We were scheduled to play doubles, but someone couldn't make it, so Borotra and I played singles instead, altering the rules so we could compete on equal terms despite the considerable difference in our ages. Here's how we went about it.

I won the toss and elected to serve. For the first point, I served into the right service court as always. (We made no deviations from the service rules at all, in fact.) But Borotra, according to the system we devised, was required to make a cross-court return. The entire left half of my court was out of bounds (you have to imagine the half court line extending to the base line), but he could hit into the right-hand alley. In other words, I was defending the right half of a doubles court. Similarly, all *my* shots were required to be cross-court. The second point was played the same way except reversed; we used the left half of each court rather than the right side, but again making every shot cross-court.

For the third point, we required that all shots be down the line. The serve was delivered in the normal cross-court manner, but then the action shifted to my left court and Borotra's right, just as if the full court had been split down the middle. For the fourth point, we did the same thing on the opposite side; my left court and Borotra's right were out of bounds. Then we started all over again by playing the fifth point cross-court. And so on.

It amazed me to discover how effectively this system reduces the younger player's usual advantages. Borotra, who has always liked to rush to the net, could do so this way without great risk of being passed because my angle for passing shots was narrow. On a full court, at his age, he couldn't have gotten away with it. Also, since the area of the target is smaller, you must hit the ball more carefully to keep it in bounds—which naturally means it will carry less speed. This, too, is to the older man's advantage. I managed to beat Borotra, but it was a very even match, and I suspect that using these rules he could have given a good account of himself against a player as young as Clark Graebner even—the difference in their ages being something like forty years.

Older players are often better than young ones, of course. Perhaps you know the story about the country club champion whose opponent failed to show up one day, so he asked an older fellow, forty-five maybe, if he'd like to substitute. The older man beat his brains out. The champ couldn't understand it, but his opponent said, "That's nothing. You should see my father play." So a match was arranged between the champ and this guy's father, and once more the older man won. "That's nothing," he said, "you should see *my* father play—and he's a ninety-five-year-old diabetic." So another match was arranged, but grandpa didn't show up. He sent his grandson to express his regrets. The old man couldn't make it because he was getting married that day. "Why does he want to get married?" asked the champ. "It isn't that he *wants* to," said the grandson. "He *has* to."

Don't sell us old men too short.

Chapter 11

THE ACCOUTERMENTS OF THE GAME

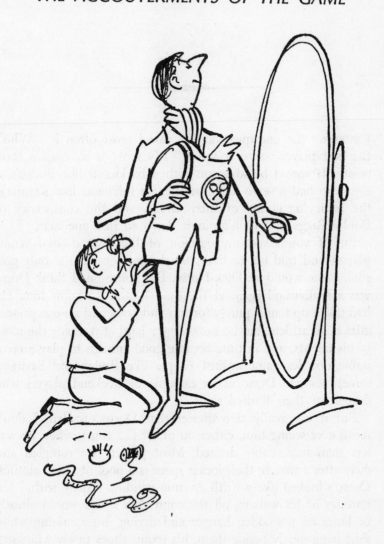

I suppose the one question I'm asked most often is, "Who's the best player you ever faced?" My reply is an evasive composite. It would be someone with a backhand like Budge's, I say, who had a serve like Gonzales', a forehand like Kramer's, the retrieving ability of Bitsy Grant, and the consistency of Bobby Riggs. I couldn't pin it down to just one man.

But if you asked my opinion of the best *dressed* tennis player—and told me to limit my choice to men—the only possible name would be Dick Dorso. By profession, I think Dorso was a Hollywood agent at the time I came to know him. He had taken up tennis purely for fun and possessed no exceptional gifts as an athlete, but he worked very hard at it, made the most of his talents, and in time became good enough to play a creditable doubles game against people like Budge and Savitt. I sometimes cite Dorso as an example to weekend players who despair of their limited skills.

But it was really as a dresser that Dorso excelled. I don't recall ever seeing him, either on or off the court, when he was less than impeccably dressed. Most players are rumpled and dirty after a match; their locker space is a pool of soiled clothes. Dorso's looked like a Fifth Avenue window display within ten minutes of his walking off the court. His shorts would already be hung on a wooden hanger and drying, his sparkling white shirt lying neatly beside them, his tennis shoes newly whitened.

Dorso himself would be nattily decked out in whatever latest style fit the occasion. His taste was as sharp as the crease in his trousers, which he kept like a razor by never sitting down. I mean *literally* never sitting down. At a party, he'd spend the whole evening on his feet rather than risk wrinkling his pants. I've known some other players who were pretty snazzy dressers, or anyhow gave a great deal of thought to their clothes. Dick Savitt carried enough luggage for a trip around the world to a tournament that lasted three days. But Dorso is up there in a class by himself. He even wears a foulard handkerchief in his pajamas. Dorso now operates a fancy boutique in Beverly Hills.

Athletes, as a rule, are terrible dressers. Their taste in clothes is simply atrocious. I forget who Jim Murray, the sports columnist, was referring to when he said that his costume "looks like a combination of the Aurora Borealis and a gangster's funeral wreath," but dozens of possibilities come to mind. Tennis players and cricket players were once the exceptions, but they, too, have lately grown sloppy. Until recently, one of the prettiest sights in all sports was of the American Davis Cup team walking proudly onto the court in their glistening white tennis outfits. The sharpness of their dress gave the matches that followed a genuine sense of occasion. But now? Well, now they straggle out in ugly sweat pants, which they wear these days to warm up in. When I say they look exactly like basketball players, I assure you I don't intend that as a compliment.

But I guess it could be a lot worse than it is. At least they haven't dropped to the sartorial level of golfers—down there with Tommy Bolt, who wears rose-and-black plaid golf shoes, and various other Beau Brummells of the links who look as if they got dressed in the dark. I don't know any tennis players with a wardrobe like Doug Sanders'. Sanders, you may have noticed, favors the sunburst style of dress. One of his typical golfing ensembles is fire-engine red from top to bottom—red shirt, red trousers, red belt, red socks, right down to flaming red shoes. With Doug's build—he's physically tall and thin—he looks as if he's on his way to a Halloween party disguised as a bottle of ketchup.

"White is right" is the old rule for tennis attire, and that tradition is based on sound reasons. White reflects sunlight and helps you keep cool. It offers less distraction to the eye than bright colors and thereby aids a player's concentration. It makes an esthetically pleasing picture when both players, or all four of them, are completely dressed in white. White clothes are also considered more healthful—no dye to get in blistered feet, for instance.

But of course we're now living in the full-color era, and traditions are toppling all around. Actually, the move toward colored tennis clothing isn't very recent. Mulloy made the suggestion, a good many years ago, that if tennis shirts were any color other than white, the ball would stand out against them better. His suggestion was coolly ignored at the time, but nowadays colored shirts are all the vogue—not the psychedelic hues a golfer might wear, but delicate and tasteful pastels. Commercially instigated, at the most recent U. S. Open at Forest Hills, Arthur Ashe, Stan Smith, and Bob Lutz were among the players who wore pastel shirts on the court. Pale yellow and light blue are the most popular shades, not only for shirts but for warm-up sweaters too. Several of my own sweaters are pastel, in fact, although I still prefer all-white tennis shirts. It's a matter of personal taste. As far as the USLTA is concerned, either white or pastel is acceptable. But any gaudier color is strictly taboo except when employed very sparingly—in a red-and-blue trim around your collar, for example, or a thin ring around the top of your socks.

Tennis clothes, like any other kind of apparel, should be functional and at the same time attractive. In the days before the outbreak of the Second World War, the emphasis was on a modest appearance. Women played in dresses that reached at least to the knee, and men took the court wearing flannels or "longs" to conceal their unbeautiful legs. Many still wear them for that reason today and deserve to be applauded for good taste. Others find them useful in cool weather, of course. But longs are uncomfortable on those hot afternoons when most tennis matches are played. They greatly restrict movement and they absorb a lot of sweat, so that you seem to be carrying ten extra pounds. We can all thank Bunny Austin, the fine English player, for introducing shorts to the game. Bunny was the first man to wear them at Wimbledon—about 1936, I believe—and the fashion quickly spread around the world.

Take my advice, men, and make sure your tennis shorts fit properly. (Gals who wear shorts instead of skirts should do likewise.) You'll look a lot better, and you'll probably get more freedom of movement. I'm appalled to see a man walk onto the court in a pair of shorts that are obviously too tight. (With women, if they're pretty, I'm more tolerant.) I know he isn't comfortable, his movement is restricted, and the tugging and pulling he's forced to resort to are enormously unsightly and embarrassing. It's only slightly better to see a man with thin legs and baggy pants—the Archie Moore style of attire. Remember his big boxing trunks that reached almost to his knees? Men's tennis shorts are available with a three- or five-inch inseam, but for me I prefer a minimum of seven. If you want to wear a bikini, go swimming.

Tennis shirts should also be sufficiently large, though not loose enough to flap in the breeze. Tightness in the shoulder will hamper your swing, and if the tail barely reaches the level of your waist, you'll be constantly pulling it out. One of the attractive features of the very fine LaCoste shirts is that the tail is extra long. Even golfers keep their shirt tails tucked in. Many shirts today are made of miracle fabrics, as are the majority of the better shorts. If you take them into the shower with you after a match, they'll be dry again, and clean, within hours. Hang them on wooden hangers to avoid rust marks.

What you wear on your feet when playing tennis is important. Unless you play on grass courts, which are softer than the others, the way to prevent blisters is with two pairs of socks—an inner layer of something like nylon or thin cotton, then the thicker wool socks on top. Be sure to turn the tops down so they don't resemble kneesocks. And always wear both pairs when trying on new tennis shoes because a good fit is very important.

Lightweight, low-cut shoes made of canvas are the easiest to lug around the court. The best shoe to wear is the lightest one that feels comfortable. Heavier models that rise above the ankle feel like lead after a half hour of tennis. These higher shoes are sometimes called basketball shoes, but actually most basketball players—the pros, at least—now wear "tennis shoes," and for the same reason you should, because they're so much lighter. On grass or cement or asphalt or wood, the so-called "deck" shoe with a herringbone tread will give you superior traction. But if you're playing on a surface where sand or bits of gravel might stick within the spaces of a herringbone bottom, your soles should be crepe or smoothly molded (no tread). Whichever kind you wear, your shoes should be white, and they should have a built-up innersole and cushioned heel. And for heaven's sake, *keep* them white. Nothing makes a tennis player look more like a slob than a grubby pair of shoes. Some types you can toss into a washing machine. Others you must clean with shoe whitener. Don Budge made it a practice, after every match he played, even in an important tournament like Wimbledon, of immediately whitening his tennis shoes before he did anything else.

Wearing a hat on the court is good judgment, especially on a hot afternoon in strong sunlight. The original type of tennis hat, the beret, worn in France, though it offers some protection to the top of your head, provides very little shade for the eyes.

A visor, which some tennis players prefer, does the latter but not the former. Baseball-type caps with long peaks are often worn, but my personal favorite is still the floppy Australian sun hat with the turned-down brim all the way around. It covers your head and keeps the sun from your eyes, and it's roomy enough to put cabbage leaves under. No, I'm being serious. I often wrap four or five cabbage leaves around some ice cubes and stick them under my hat during the change of sides. Try it. It keeps you cool in hot weather.

Other players shun hats but wear Indian-style headbands, which at least keep the perspiration from their eyes. Headbands are especially popular with the hippie-style hairdos that a number of world-class players now affect—Ray Moore, Tom Koch, and Torben Ulrich, for example. They wear their hair as long as a girl's.

A sweatlet around your wrist serves a similar purpose. It prevents perspiration from running down your arm onto the hand that holds the racket. Some players wear two sweatlets and use the one around their left arm to wipe off their forehead or right hand with—which is certainly more attractive than hanging a towel from your shorts like the center in a football game.

Some players must acquire good taste in clothes while to others it seems to come naturally. Fred Perry was such a man. Perry, a top amateur in the mid-1930s, strutted onto the court with such elegance and bearing that he instinctively evoked the aura of top dog. It was an unconscious psyching tactic. Don Budge was one of the players who gave little thought to clothes until Perry's example impressed their importance on him. Then Don became a snappy dresser too.

Bobby Riggs, in his early days, looked scruffy on the court. He didn't give two hoots what clothes he wore. But then he went to Wimbledon in 1939 and fell under the influence of the people from Simpson's, the imposing clothing emporium in Piccadilly, who made the most of having a rough diamond to work with. When Bobby emerged, his rag-tag garb was gone, and he was handsomely attired in stylish Daks shorts, a smart tailored shirt complete with crest and initials, and a glistening white blazer with the United States shield. He won that year at Wimbledon, and then came home to play a tournament at Seabright. Bitsy Grant, who noticed Riggs's fancy new clothes, tried to psych him into a fit of self-consciousness. "What kind of chance do *I* have," Bitsy moaned, "with my ninety-eight-cent T-shirt and public park shorts against someone dandied up the way *you* are?" But Riggs merely grinned; he wasn't bothered in the slightest. He had reached a new level of confidence where for the first time he genuinely felt like a champion because at last he looked like one.

Riggs is still out there beating everyone in sight, but Perry quit playing to pursue his love of clothes and is now one of England's leading designers of tennis outfits. One of Fred's competitors is another former great, a Frenchman by the name of René LaCoste, who uses as his emblem a small crocodile. (LaCoste, in his playing days, was sometimes called "le crocodile" for the way in which he moved on the court.) He has now created several styles of dresses, all very chic with simple lines.

Teddy Tinling, although good enough to play four times at Wimbledon, never approached the great heights as a player that Perry and LaCoste achieved. But Teddy surpasses their fame today as a designer of tennis clothes. He makes clothes for both sexes, but his outfits for women account for his world-wide acclaim. Even if the name Teddy Tinling fails to ring a bell, you've undoubtedly heard of his creations. He first drew wide notice in 1949 as the designer of Gussie Moran's lace panties. Shortly after that came the peekaboo outfit—*broderie anglaise* with patterns cut through it—that both Gussie and Beverly Baker wore to play in. In 1955, for Italy's Lea Pericoli, Teddy fashioned tennis' first petticoat, a pink one. (Tinling loves colors and has been bucking the "white is right" rule for something like twenty-five years.) The gold lamé underpants he made for Karol Fageros were followed by an assortment of bright-colored outfits for Brazil's Maria Bueno; both her underpants and skirt lining were done in vivid colors—in one case, purple and green. The establishment howled to high heaven about that one, possibly because the colors of the All England Club, which runs Wimbledon, are also purple and green. What was Teddy doing—poking fun?

At the most recent "eve of Wimbledon" fashion show in Hurlingham, Tinling gave the tennis world a glimpse of what's to come. We ain't seen nothin' yet. In the future, he hopes to dress "his" girls, as he calls them, in ballerina outfits adorned with pink rosebuds; purple satin dresses trimmed with feathered pigeons; knee-length maxi-skirts over lacy blue tights; and a "Star-Spangled Banner" suit for American players that looks vaguely like a desecrated flag. So far no hint of a topless design but he has threatened a see-through tennis blouses.

Tinling says his fashions are all based on one rule: "a simple line following the figure, with frills from the hip down." Many women leap to them as to a gown by Dior. Others, though, consider them too frivolous and frilly, and opt for more workmanlike patterns. Billie Jean King and Margaret Court, for example, from the current top echelon of world-rated players, stick to simple shirt-and-skirt combinations. Predictably, Tinling disparages their choice. He's particularly critical of Mrs. Court's clothes, possibly because she once wore Tinling dresses then later decided not to. He said of her before her latest Wimbledon outing: "She'll be in rags as usual. Shirt and skirt. Four pounds —ten dollars—off any rack."

For myself, I'm reluctant to take sides in the matter. I certainly enjoy seeing women fetchingly dolled up. But I could also make an argument for plainness. On the tennis court, a girl's attractiveness should not be disconcerting. This especially holds true in a mixed doubles match. As it is, men have trouble keeping their mind on the game. If women start wearing dresses that distract us even more . . . well, as a man, I don't consider that *fair*.

Clothes make the man, they say, but it takes more to make a tennis player. During my earliest years on the circuit, Don Budge was less than the best-dressed player but he was the undisputed giant of the game. In 1938 he became the first man in history to win the Grand Slam of tennis, a feat that wasn't duplicated until 1962, when Rod Laver also accomplished it—as he did again in 1969. The Grand Slam consists of winning the national singles championships of Australia, France, England, and the United States, the four most coveted titles in the world, all in a single year. Three of these championships are contested on grass. The French title is the only exception.

Grass is a fast surface ideally suited to Don's style. He played a hard, driving game with lots of power. His opponents got the feeling—at least I always did—of standing in a trench ten feet behind the base line and being mistaken for the target on a rifle range. Every time you looked, another bullet.

Budge at his best was invincible on grass. But on a clay court, Don could be had. Clay is a much slower surface than grass, and it diminishes the effectiveness of raw power like Budge's, consequently favoring a guy like Bitsy Grant, who lacked power but was an exceptional retriever. Playing Bitsy, you'd hit a shot you thought sure was a winner—and probably on a grass court it *would* be a winner—but on clay, which gives a scrambler more time to do his work, he'd chase it down and hit it back again. Someone with Budge's style could get demoralized. Don would unleash one of his blistering backhands, the kind he was accustomed to wrapping up points with, and Bitsy would run it down and lob it back. Inevitably, Don would hit the next one even harder. Bitsy would turn tail and manage somehow to catch up to it. Back it would come again. After this kind of thing went on for a while, Don might become exasperated, toss aside the percentages, and risk shots that were too big a gamble. Or else he might exhaust his energy. It's *work* to hit a tennis ball as hard as Don Budge did, and as often as Bitsy Grant *made* him hit it. Bitsy would then take command of the action, because he could run all afternoon without tiring. Don—who seldom had to—couldn't. He invested most of his strength in powdering the ball. As often as not, Grant won the match.

It does make a difference what surface you play on. If you're blessed with the explosive talents of a Budge, stick to the fastest courts you can find. But if your tennis skills are somewhat less impressive than Don's—and I feel fairly confident in guessing that they are—a slower court is much to your advantage. Not only will it heighten your chances of winning, it will add to your enjoyment of the game.

Let's talk awhile about the different court surfaces and the various characteristics of each.

Certainly the most difficult surface to play on is an indoor court made of wood. First of all, the fact that you're playing inside means the lighting is less than perfect. A tennis ball traveling at a hundred miles an hour—Gonzales' serve was once timed at 120—can be hard to follow even in sunlight. Under artificial lights, it's sheer murder. Besides that, wood is an extremely hard surface; there's practically no "give" to it at all. The combination poses a very definite problem; a ball hit with pace can bound past before you see it. The use of colored tennis balls sometimes helps a little (yellow is the color most frequently used), but not a tremendous amount. Even top professionals trust to instinct and luck. There's simply no *way* for a limited player to give a good account of himself on wood.

Fortunately, indoor courts no longer have to be wood. Several synthetic surfaces are available today and can be tailored to any speed you desire. These surfaces are also portable. Touring pros lay them down on basketball courts, then roll them up again after each evening's matches and carry them along to the next place. On top of that, they can be used either indoors or out—one place in the summertime, another in the winter— and are thereby making tennis a truly year-round activity for the player of modest skills.

Another new development I'm happy to see is the use of plastic bubbles. They're booming all over the country. The bubbles are inflated with air like a zeppelin to protect the court from inclement weather. Some of them are just big enough to cover one court and cost about $20,000. Others are big enough for a polo field, with a price tag of maybe $100,000. What I like about them is that they let more people play more tennis year-round, thus adding to the popularity of the sport.

Of the nonsynthetic surfaces that are used out of doors, the trickiest to play on is grass. Weekenders who seldom have occasion to play on grass—there are relatively few grass courts in this country because upkeep is difficult and therefore expensive—sometimes think grass, because it's soft, is also slow. Actually, most grass courts are very fast indeed. The grass is cut short, about a quarter-inch high, and the ground underneath is kept hard. "Cement with fuzz on it" is Vic Seixas' description of the center court at Wimbledon, the finest grass court in the world.

A game played on grass is esthetically pleasing. The white clothes and white ball against the soothing green background makes a very appealing picture. Players have no difficulty following the ball, and a grass court is easy on the legs; there's a spring to it that harder courts lack.

One characteristic that makes grass hard to play on is the likelihood of getting bad bounces. Even at a place like Forest Hills, you can count on a couple weird bounces every set, because the surface of grass courts is uneven. You can never be quite certain how the ball will shoot off it, and when a crazy hop deprives you of a critical point, your morale and concentration can be ruined. The single exception is Wimbledon, where the courts are maintained with such meticulous care that the problem of bad bounces is negligible. Budge, when asked how he liked England, said, "Great, I didn't get a bad bounce all the while I was there."

The other thing that makes grass a tricky surface to play on is that the ball skids along it and bounces low. The angle of reflection is not equal, even approximately, to the angle of incidence. In other words, it isn't like playing on wood—or on concrete or asphalt or any other hard surface—where a ball that strikes the court at, say, a 20-degree angle will rebound at that same angle, or close to it. On grass, a shot will skid along the surface a way (picking up grass stains that make the ball heavy), then leave it at a much reduced angle. Consequently, on a grass court you spend more time hitting up. You get fewer opportunities to return on straight lines balls that rebound higher than the net. A retriever is at a great disadvantage on grass because the ball moves by so fast and stays so low.

Concrete and asphalt can be considered together because their properties as court surfaces are closely similar. Both have the advantage of being easy to maintain, which accounts for the great popularity they enjoy among officials who budget funds for public courts. Their hard, gritty surfaces are tough on tennis balls, but you shouldn't get many bad bounces. The ball comes off quickly at a higher angle than off grass—though at a lower angle than off clay. Playing on these surfaces is rough on the legs. Once after a tournament on cement in Los Angeles my legs hurt so much I couldn't play for two weeks. It's the same constant pounding that plagues basketball players. But the greatest disadvantage for the weekend tennis player is that cement and asphalt courts are just too fast—even if the cement has been grained to slow the bounce, or rubber has been put in the asphalt for the same purpose. He doesn't have the "big" game they favor. Even world-class players unaccustomed to these surfaces often find the speed too much to cope with. In the 1969 Davis Cup Challenge Round, in Cleveland, the United States routed Romania without the loss of a match—first, in my opinion, because our team was superior, but also because the courts at Harold T. Clark Stadium, which have a hard, asphaltic composition surface, were treated for extra speed. The Romanians were accustomed to playing on clay; their home courts are among the world's slowest. On asphalt, they couldn't keep up.

Clay or composition courts, or *en touts cas* or synthetics, are in my opinion better for most players. *En touts cas* is a surface made of crushed red brick, more often seen in Europe than over here. Clay and composition are usually thought of together because both are normally slow courts, but in only one sense: the ball bounces higher and more slowly off these surfaces than off any other kind used for tennis. But this tends to make the game itself much faster and more interesting by minimizing the risk of those dull swat-and-fetch-it matches in which you stand around and watch the ball streak by. A player who hustles can return more shots on clay. Long, exciting rallies are sustained. You can think of the difference between a clay court and grass as approximately two steps. On clay, a good retriever can get his racket on a ball that he couldn't get nearer than two steps from on grass. That's a very considerable difference indeed, and almost always it will work to the advantage of the player who lacks blinding power. It defuses the "big" game effectively. Even top professionals are wary, on clay, about following their serve to the net.

Perhaps I should note here that my advice to weekend players that their game will be better on slow courts than fast ones is no reflection of my own luck on either. My skills as a player were about equally suited to one type of surface as another. If anything, I have a sentimental fondness for grass, since most of the trophies I've managed to win, and the majority of the thirty-five national championships, were in tournaments played on grass. But I insist that for the typical now-and-then player, the slower the court, the better.

Another of the suggestions I sometimes set forth at variance with what I happen to practice myself is that beginning players start with metal rackets. Personally, I still prefer wood. I've grown so accustomed to wood, I suppose, that anything else feels strange. Any veteran player who has a similar reaction should stick to whatever he's used to—assuming, of course, that it works pretty well.

But I've tried the metal rackets, both steel and aluminum— tested them pretty thoroughly, as a matter of fact—and in many ways they're superior to wood. For one thing, a metal racket cuts more smoothly through the air; it offers less wind resistance. That means you can get it back into position to swing faster, and also give the stroke itself more speed. Then, too, in spite of its relative lightness, the metal racket seems to me sturdier. It won't splinter or warp, and I doubt if you could break one, although hurling it at a net post in anger might bend it.

In contrast to the face of the wood racket, which is oval, most of the metal rackets have a circular face. As a result, when the ball hits the center of the strings—what tennis players some-times refer to as "the sweet spot"—the metal racket imparts more speed and pace; the ball leaves the strings with more "stuff" on it. Closer to the rim, though, this advantage dis-appears, and a ball hit off-center might pursue a wayward path. The wood racket allows greater control. It's something like the difference between piloting a jet and piloting a low-speed Piper Cub. The former, if you know how to fly it with precision, will respond with greater performance; the latter is more for-giving of errors. So if you think you can learn how to handle the metal racket, I advise you to give it a try.

The choice between metal and wood comes first, but the selection of a racket involves much more than that. Weight, balance, grip size, handle surface, stringing—all these considerations enter in.

Let's start with the question of grip size. The way to find what grip size your racket should have is to "shake hands" with several on display in the pro shop, models with handles of different circumferences—just hold them in the regular eastern grip—and see which one feels most comfortable. Handle sizes start at about four and a quarter inches and go up at eighth-inch intervals to five inches. It's sensible to sample all sizes. Women naturally tend to pick smaller handle sizes, but don't be swayed by averages or by what another player might prefer. Choose the one that feels best in *your* hand.

The same rule applies, of course, to the weight of the racket. Some players like to use an extremely heavy racket and others choose the lightest they can find. John Bromwich, the Aus-tralian, had considerable success with a racket that weighed only about twelve and three-fourths ounces, which is even lighter than most women would select. Children just beginning should use very light rackets—eleven and a half or twelve ounces. From that point, weights go up at intervals of a quarter of an ounce to fifteen ounces or so. Women's rackets average about thirteen and a quarter ounces, men's perhaps half an ounce more. But again, don't allow yourself to be ruled by statistics. What matters is to find the weight for *you*. Begin with the lightest racket in the shop; just pick it up and swing it a few times. Then try the next heavier weight, then the next, and right on up the line. When you get to a racket that feels heavy in your hand, drop down a quarter ounce, and that's your weight. So long as it's comfortable, the heavier the racket, the more pace you can impart to the ball.

Length presents no problems since most rackets are the same: twenty-seven inches (most metal rackets are slightly shorter, but wider except, of course, for special children's models). But they vary from one another in balance. Some rackets are noticeably heavy-in-the-head, others light-in-the-head, still others even. You can easily determine how a racket is balanced by seeing which way it tips, if at all, when you place a finger underneath its mid-point. Most top-rated players use evenly balanced rackets, and weekenders, in this instance, should copy them. The other kinds are more difficult to manage.

The decision of how you should have your racket strung involves three related questions: What material should be used? What size? And how tight? My advice to casual players is that they use light fifteen-gauge nylon at anywhere from fifty-four to fifty-eight pounds, which is the medium tension range. Rackets strung with lamb gut give a slightly better bite, and are therefore the preference of most serious players, but nylon has the advantage of being much longer lasting and more resistant to deterioration in damp weather. Nylon, in short, is the economical choice, and without being grossly inferior in performance. The same reasoning supports the use of fifteen-gauge thickness. Thinner strings are used by most top-ranking players, but thinner strings tend to break sooner. As for tension, it's a choice of control versus speed, and a middle course seems a sensible compromise. Vic Seixas was successful with a very tight racket—sixty-five pounds of tension, I believe—so that his shots flew off like bullets, but sometimes wildly. John Bromwich, on the other hand, had his rackets strung so loosely they reminded his opponents of snowshoes— forty-six pounds, I'd estimate. He sacrificed pace for great control.

You can use any material you happen to like the feel of

to cover your racket handle. One of the most popular choices is leather, either genuine leather or the simulated kind, though some players prefer cork, and others like friction tape because it gives them a stickier grip. A few have been known to use ordinary toweling, presumably to absorb perspiration. Don Budge is among those who use nothing at all; his hand enjoys the feel of plain wood.

Once you've bought a racket, it pays to take care of it. Keep it in a cover to reduce the risk of damage, and in a press to prevent warping if it's wood; metal rackets don't require presses. Leaving it outside on the grass overnight or throwing it around the court in anger is obviously ill-advised. Personally, such abuse of tennis rackets makes me cringe. My own are treated like Stradivarius violins. Excessive heat or moisture can ruin the strings, so don't store your racket in the car trunk. Think of it as an expensive camera loaded with film or as a favorite phonograph record; the danger posed by heat is much the same. If you're playing in the rain and get your racket strings wet, sprinkle a little bit of talcum powder on them to reduce the possibility of damage. And remember that a racket is personal equipment. Asking to borrow someone else's is a no-no.

The choice of tennis balls presents an obvious problem: there are dozens of different kinds on the market. Some of them are advertised for all-purpose use, while others are designed for a particular surface or perhaps for some special condition. There are grass court balls and clay court balls and heavy-duty balls for asphalt or cement (the hard, gritty surface tends to wear the fuzz off quickly) and balls of bright colors for use on indoor courts—even balls especially fashioned for high altitudes. The dilemma of which kind is best suited for your purposes can be resolved by nothing better than trial and error. The more expensive balls usually last longer than the cheaper ones; you end up getting roughly what you pay for.

When should old tennis balls be replaced by a new batch? It depends on what kind you're using and what surface you're playing on—also on how finicky you are. Playing with a dead ball or a water-logged ball is obviously no fun; the whole rhythm of the sport is upset. You're probably familiar with the old rule of thumb: A tennis ball should bounce at least as high as your waist if you hold it over your head and let it drop on a hard surface. If it doesn't, the time has come to throw it out. And even if it passes this standard test, a ball with no fuzz on, or discolored by grass stains, should also be tossed out of play. On the other hand, you're simply throwing money out the window if you discard a ball that still has good mileage in it. Which doesn't keep a lot of players from doing so. Some people have what amounts to a craving for new tennis balls; they'd like to open another can for every point. I recently was one of the players in a short two-set match in which twenty-four new balls were put in play. Such extravagance is completely unnecessary; we could easily have gotten along as well on six. But at least the guy who wanted them had agreed to foot the bill. The *worst* thing you can do is to insist on new balls and then forget about paying your share.

Maybe it's a throwback to my public court years, but I hate to see a ball that's still usable thrown away. As a kid, I used to gather up other player's rejects and rejuvenate them by sandpapering to raise the fuzz a little bit. They played almost as well as brand new ones.

Chapter 12

THE FAMILY THAT PLAYS TOGETHER

BACK IN Cincinnati, during my first years on the circuit, there were two brothers who partnered each other in doubles and were good enough to get invited to a lot of out-of-town tournaments. Each time they loaded up the car and took off again, the neighbors used to comment on how nice it must be for a family to share an interest in tennis. What could be more pleasant than a partnership of brothers, traveling together all around the country?

I suspect that these neighbors never saw the boys play. I saw them often, and my view of them was different. Never have I known tennis partners to fight more than they did. Constantly yelling insults and complaints back and forth, blaming each other bitterly for every lost point, they sounded like a couple of characters out of *Who's Afraid of Virginia Woolf*. Once, I remember, they drove East to play a tournament at Randalls Island, in New York. Well, one brother started to poach. The other, after issuing some strongly worded warnings, announced that if it happened just one more time, that would be the end of their partnership. It happened one more time and, true to his word, he immediately stalked off the court. He climbed into their car and drove back to Cincinnati, leaving his brother stranded.

Tennis within the family doesn't *have* to be like that. In my own case, I immensely enjoy playing with my sons, and

I feel pretty certain they reciprocate that pleasure. I'm merely pointing out that it *can* be like that. Consider yourself forewarned.

And the more seriously you take the game, of course, the greater the risk becomes. Clark Graebner, who is currently ranked second in the country, can serve as a perfect example. He and I and Carole, his wife, were discussing it out at Forest Hills recently. Off court, Graebner is an agreeable fellow who seldom says an unpleasant word. But with a racket in his hand, he's so intent upon winning that he lacerates his partners with cutting criticism. And he's much less inhibited when it's someone in his family than when his partner is a relative stranger. That's how it often is with tennis players on the court; they treat the people they're closest to worst. When Graebner and his dad were playing father-and-son doubles, Clark often bit his father's head off with his comments, railing at him for every missed shot. And with Carole, Clark's wife, the problem was doubled because Carole is a top-ranking player in her own right, once rated fourth in the world among women. When they competed as a husband-and-wife doubles team, Carole barked at Clark as much as Clark barked at Carole.

Personally, I'm guilty of the other poor attitude that often afflicts families with more than one player. I fret like the stereotype of the Little League parent. I'm too partisan a rooter when my sons are on the court. I frequently lose my perspective. If a linesman makes a bad call against Pike or Peter, I feel like punching him in the nose. And the ironic thing is, when I'm out there myself, I've never let bad calls bother me. Being helpless on the side lines is what's frustrating. One of the trophies I'm proudest of winning is the William M. (Little Bill) Johnston Award, which is given each year to "that man player who by his character, good sportsmanship, manners, spirit of co-operation and contribution to the growth of the game ranks first in the opinion of the selection committee." That trophy is among my most valued possessions. But when I'm watching Pike or Peter in action, thinking nasty thoughts about their opponents or the officials, my conscience suggests that I surrender the award because I'm doing disrespect to the inscription. Or maybe I should do what my own parents did. My mother stayed home whenever I played, and my father always watched from behind a tree.

Aside from not embarrassing me with partisan support, my father did me another good turn when I was starting. He put me into the hands of a local player in Cincinnati who encouraged me to learn the game properly. I advise you to do the same thing for your children—or for your husband or wife, if you've married a nonplayer. It's never too late to learn.

A country club pro is often a good choice, but it isn't the only one. My own development, for instance, was with a public court supervisor. Nowadays, there are also tennis classes in the schools—usually group lessons, not private instruction, but you can learn in group lessons, and they're free. Community clinics can also be useful, even if they only last a day or so. I conduct enough of these free public clinics myself—forty or fifty in a typical year—to be convinced they do the kids a lot of good.

Wherever your youngster receives his first instruction, make sure he starts out with stroke lessons. Their purpose is to teach him the fundamentals of the game—the grip, proper footwork, weight balance, and stroke production. Since he'll never learn anything more important about the game, his instructor in this period must be competent. Not all tennis pros are. Even golfers, sad to say, are ahead of us in this regard. To qualify as a golf pro, you must meet certain standards established by the PGA —the Professional Golfers' Association. No such requirements are imposed on a tennis pro. He becomes one by proclaiming himself one. Therefore, you must scrutinize a pro's qualifications before you entrust your youngsters to his tutelage—his qualifications as a *teacher*, mind you, not necessarily as a player.

Many top instructors were only mediocre players and, conversely, many stars make lousy teachers. Basically, what it takes is a sure knowledge of fundamentals, endless patience, an ability to communicate, and a good rapport with youngsters. A devotion to simplicity is also essential. Pros who make everything sound immensely complicated are almost always phonies. They figure they have to make it sound harder than it is to give their clients the feeling that they're getting their full money's worth. Don't be taken in by that game. Tennis is indeed a difficult sport, but a first-rate teacher—of *any* subject—is the one who has the ability to reduce it to its essence and who then plugs away until the student truly grasps it.

At that point, it's time to move on to playing lessons. In a playing lesson, the pro acts as the student's opponent, stretching his ability through controlled competition (the teacher plays just slightly above the student's own level) mixed with constructive criticism. For playing lessons, you can get by with a lesser instructor. His primary function of hitting balls at the beginner within the framework of an actual tennis game is less demanding than grounding him in the basics. When Pike and Peter were in advanced learning stages, I sometimes had them play against not-so-good teachers just so they'd face a variety of styles. But I always told those pros to confine themselves to playing, not to make any comments. I didn't want them filling the boys' heads with bad advice. I would do the actual teaching.

Helping to develop a young player is rewarding—especially if it's your own offspring, but even if it isn't. Undoubtedly the best player I've groomed is Tony Trabert. Tony is another of our Cincinnati products, and his potential was obvious to me the first time I saw him play there. We worked together closely for a number of years trying to perfect his skills. I guess you could consider him my protégé. In 1953, when he won at Forest Hills, achieving the United States singles championship I had twice missed myself by losing in the finals, I was even more elated than if the triumph had been mine. And returning the Davis Cup from Australia the next year—though by that time I had become a nonplaying captain—was just as rewarding, perhaps even more so, than winning the Cup in '48 and '49, when I was myself a participant—particularly since Trabert was on the team in '54 and won in both singles and doubles.

Neither of my own sons has Traberts natural talent. In fact, they can't even beat *me* yet. Long ago I made a bargain with Pike and Peter. I told them I'd put $1000 in the bank in their name when they could beat me playing singles fair and square. They're permitted only one formal challenge each summer, and so far I've been able to win them all. But Pike, the older boy, will be twenty-one this year, and I'm afraid my Waterloo may be approaching.

Even if your kids are no more talented than mine are—and actually both of mine are pretty good for their ages, it's just that they can't handle the Old Man yet—I encourage you to spend as much time as you can with them helping them reach the limit of their skills. The effort will pay dividends for fifty or sixty years. And few things a parent can do with a youngster are so mutually satisfying. Tennis leaves other sports far behind in this respect. If you try to teach your boy or girl to ski, for example, are you fully aware of what you're letting yourself in for? Crying kids, frozen fingers, costly equipment, and maybe a couple legs wrapped in casts. Tennis, on the other hand, is *fun*.

Here are a few simple rules you should follow:

◄ Don't be overanxious to get your kids started. You might have heard the story, undoubtedly true, that Earl Buchholz, later a member of the U. S. Davis Cup team, began to play tennis at the ripe old age of three and entered his first tournament at six. I beg you not to take that as a precedent. Buchholz was phenomenally precocious as an athlete, literally one player in a million. Most kids that age can barely lift a racket—even the rackets they now make for children. And trying to play tennis before you can handle a racket is a good way to get discouraged and lose interest. Wait until your son or daughter gives some indication of wanting to learn. Usually, it won't be until the age of ten or so—maybe eleven or twelve for smaller kids. Believe me, that isn't too late to begin. I was thirteen when I first swung a racket.

◄ Whenever you can, use the buddy system. Work with two youngsters instead of one. They can serve as opponents and toss balls for each other, and they'll develop a competitive companionship that will stimulate both players' development. My own boys, whose ages are two years apart, were taught that way and are the fiercest of rivals. After Peter lost to Pike at a club tournament last summer, he ran into my old adversary, Frank Parker. "My brother always bugs me," Peter complained. "He psychs me and I can never seem to beat him."

"The next time you play him," Parker advised, "move to a hotel room the night before the match. He can't psych you if you're not around the house. Hang his picture in the room and throw darts at it."

◄ Be patient. After you've explained how a stroke is produced, your boy or girl will need to try it thousands of times before the faintest glimmer of proficiency appears. Don't expect too much of him too soon. During this period, the best thing you can do is simply toss tennis balls at him by the hour. Take a whole bushel basketful onto the court—old balls are just as good as new ones for this purpose—and from a distance of ten or a dozen feet, throw them underhand to a spot where he can hit them. At first, he probably won't do very well. Occasionally he might miss the ball entirely. Don't allow these temporary failures to upset him. Just toss another ball and let him try again. When your basket is empty, refill it and start over—reminding yourself, if boredom threatens, that this is how champions are made. As he improves, you can move to the other side of the net and start hitting the balls gently instead of tossing them.

◄ Introduce an element of fun into the proceedings. Practice, especially for younger players, can be drudgery if you don't jazz it up a bit. Use whatever devices you can think of. One common trick is to practice strokes to music; besides being pleasant to listen to, music encourages a smooth, flowing rhythm. Tiresome routines can be turned into games. Rather than just practicing a sequence of strokes, do it, when the youngster is an appropriate age, within the format of Simon Says or Follow the Leader. An element of competition can also stir interest. Toss a hundred tennis balls to each of two beginners and see which one returns the greater number. Anything that makes practice more attractive is good.

◄ Proceed slowly. I've said it before and I'll say it again: Anyone who hopes to be a winning tennis player must practice the fundamentals of the game. The best time to do it—the only time really—is in the earliest stages of learning. A good tennis teacher delays the next lesson until the last one is very well in hand. No virtue is attached to leaping ahead. Tennis isn't grade school, where a kid is thought stupid if he stays in first grade for three years. In tennis, first grade is where winners are made, and only future losers rush through. Anything omitted from a player's early schooling, or passed over quickly before it manages to sink in, will haunt him later on. As beginners, most top players spent month after month doing nothing but grooving their swing, usually with their teacher present to make them do it right. Clark Graebner says of his father, who taught him to play, "He hit balls at me for hundreds of thousands of hours, as if he were a Ball-Boy machine." Tennis is a difficult sport to learn; rushing it makes it impossible. Few players master it young.

I do remember one boy, though, who came to see me in New York City when I was the captain of our Junior Davis

Cup team. He told me he wanted to play on the squad, and I asked him to describe his talents.

"Well, my forehand," he said, "is a little better than Kramer's. I use an eastern grip, and I can hit it either cross-court or down the line, with either topspin or backspin, and I never miss."

"Great," I said. "What about your backhand?"

"I move my grip a one-eighth turn and hit with a little more power than Rosewall," he said. "I can give it overspin or underspin, hit deep or short, cross-court or down the line."

"You sound like the kind of player we've been looking for," I told him. "Is your volleying pretty good?"

"Oh yeah," he answered. "I can punch it or hit drop-volleys to any part of the court, deep or short."

"What about your serve?"

"I hit it pretty hard," he said. "Gonzales' serve was timed at a hundred twenty miles an hour. Mine goes a hundred twenty-three. And I always get the first serve in."

"You sound like the perfect player," I said. "Don't you have any weaknesses at all?"

"Just one," he replied. "I tell lies."

◄ Subordinate formal competition to practice. Actually playing tennis is unquestionably more fun, but for a beginner's first six months or so—until he has the rudiments firmly under control—constant repetitive practice is more useful. The ratio I suggest is roughly two-to-one: two hours of practice for each hour of competition.

◄ Emphasize his accomplishments; make light of his errors. Learning to play tennis can be a discouraging experience for even the most promising youngster. He needs all the moral support he can get to offset the feeling that, despite his hard effort, he'll never do *any*thing right. No sport I know of is so disheartening to beginners; thousands give it up almost immediately. But for those who stick it out, the rewards in later years will more than justify these early trials.

◄ Don't exert any unreasonable pressure. The Little League parent, like the Jewish mother, has become a stereotype in modern American folklore and is found just as frequently in tennis as in baseball. I wish I had a dollar for every kid I've seen made miserable by the presence on the side lines of an overzealous parent. By all means, encourage your offspring to play tennis; support them; help them; urge them to do their best. But beyond that, let them relax and have fun. No parent's dreams ever made a player a champion. The player's *own* desire to be a winner is what counts. If he wants to make the necessary sacrifices, he should make them voluntarily at a later age, when he's old enough to know what he's doing.

◄ Tailor the game to the kid's size and age. A ten-year-old youngster can't cover a whole tennis court and it's silly to make him try. When the players are beginners under twelve or thirteen, why not move the base lines in three or four feet and then cut the court in half—use only the left side or the right? Rallies will be longer and the kids will have more fun. When they first start to compete, they'll double-fault often. Don't make it cost them a point. Give them an additional serve each time, and let it be a forehand off a bounce. And since this mini-court won't be divided into left and right sides anyhow, make it legal for all serves to land anywhere over the net in front of the service line.

◄ Stop at the first sign of dwindling interest. Tennis should always be enjoyable for a youngster. Don't insist on long sessions if his attention span is short. When he says he feels like quitting, quit. Forcing him to practice after it stops being fun could sour him on the sport forever.

Eventually, your youngster will get the gist of the game, and you can allow him to practice his strokes by himself without worrying that he'll go wrong when you're not watching. At this point, he should probably have access to a backboard, the most useful of all practice devices. Maybe you can build one yourself, if none is handy. A backboard is just a wall made of concrete or wood, strong enough to hit the ball against. Ideally, it's approximately the same width as a tennis court. A painted line can represent the net. The proper way to use it is to work on one stroke at a time, grooving the swing and refining the aim—ten or fifteen minutes, say, of cross-court forehands, followed by an equal number of forehands down the line, then backhands for the same length of time. Every stroke should have a clear purpose behind it, in relationship to an imaginary game situation, and should be directed at a specific target. Just hitting the backboard any old place makes for a sloppy player.

Serves are best practiced on an actual court. Many of us, as kids, put an empty can of tennis balls at different positions on the left and right service courts and hit serves at it hour after hour. That's still the best method I know of. For beginners, though, a large box is a more suitable target; they won't miss so often and get fed up.

There are a number of good practice devices on the market, but the majority of them are intended to be sold to large groups; for one family, they're rather expensive. I'm thinking particularly of the electric Ball-Boy machine, which retails for about $400. It's similar to the Iron Mike used in baseball training camps as an automatic batting practice pitcher. You load it with balls and it fires them one by one, in accordance with the instructions you've given it.

The Re-bound Net, another Ball-Boy product (Ball-Boy, Inc., Bronxville, New York), is a nylon net stretched tightly on a frame. It comes in different sizes, with prices starting about $90 and going as high as $200. You can think of it as an enormous racket face. Unlike a backboard, it "gives" with the ball, then returns it by springing back into shape.

These devices are fine if you make enough use of them to justify the initial expense. But you can't buy your way into becoming a good player, and the amount of money you invest in teaching aids is less important than the effort you put in.

The same holds true for the services of a pro. If the time you spend with him isn't put to good advantage, you're just throwing money down the drain. Have the pro work with you on a particular weakness, or ask him to help you iron out a bad habit you've fallen into. Don't just waste his time and fool around. I'll never forget one morning I was down in the Bahamas and saw a show biz celebrity out on the tennis court at the Paradise Island Racquet Club. Pancho Gonzales was the pro there that season, and this guy had bought an hour of Pancho's time. I suppose it cost him at least fifty bucks, maybe more; Pancho is one of the best tennis players in history. So there he was, shelling out that much loot for one lesson, and what do you think he wanted Pancho to help him with? His forehand? Backhand? Improving his serve? No, sir, nothing like that. He was having Pancho teach him tricky ways to pick the ball up! You've probably seen Fancy Dans employ them on the court. One is to hold the ball against your instep with the racket head and lightly kick it into the air. Another is to strike it with the strings and get it bouncing. A third—the most likely to make impressionable blondes go "Wow!"—is to bounce it with the *edge* of the racket. Well, this guy was delighted when he learned how to do it. Pancho was understandably dismayed by it all, because the pretense that this guy was proficient with a racket would be shattered when he started to play. But maybe he never intended to play. Maybe he just wanted to stand on the side lines and impress blondes by picking up tennis balls. I'm not going to embarrass him by telling you his name, but if you've ever seen one of the girlie pageants on television, you've undoubtedly heard him sing.

Chapter 13

SCORING AND HANDICAPPING—TRADITIONAL AND OTHERWISE

GUSSIE MORAN, of lace panties fame, was unique among players on the international circuit in that she never knew what the score was—*literally* never knew it, I mean. She had no idea whose turn it was to serve or whether her side was winning. Gussie played well, and she's a smart, charming girl, but this one trait used to drive her partners crazy. Finally the great Australian star, Adrian Quist, who was playing as Gussie's partner in a mixed doubles match, decided to cure her of it. He turned to her dejectedly after they'd lost a tough point and said, "Well, that beats us, Gussie." She ran to the net with her hand outstretched, thinking to congratulate her victorious opponents, but there was nobody there to meet her— which was hardly surprising, since the match wasn't over; it stood 2–2 in the second set, in fact. This happened in the Italian championships, with Rome's largest tennis crowd of the year looking on, so you can imagine the extent of her embarrassment. It's a wonder she ever spoke to Quist again.

Yet there's something to be said for an attitude like Gussie's if you don't have much of a head for figures and if keeping score detracts from your concentration on the game or prevents you from enjoying yourself. Let someone else worry about it. Certainly that's better than the opposite tactic of spending all day in debate. "Does that make it 15–30 or 30–15?" "Why, neither —or has someone been serving in the wrong court?" "Now wait a

minute. The games stand three–two, our favor . . ." and so on
ad infinitum. It reminds me of a tableful of women at Schrafft's
dissecting a luncheon check.

Admittedly, the traditional scoring system owes no great
debt to logic. It demands some getting used to. I mean, 15, 30,
40, game—what kind of way to count is that? Why not just
1, 2, 3, 4? And what purpose is served by saying "love" instead
of "zero" or "nothing" other than to immortalize a mispronun-
ciation of the French word "l'oeuf," meaning the egg? Then
there are those people who, instead of 15, say 5—for reasons
that perhaps have something to do with the challenge of making
so bad a system worse. Maybe it would help if you forgot *all*
the numbers and used eeney, meeney, miney, moe instead. For
practical purposes, you're doing that anyhow.

The most cumbersome aspect of traditional scoring is the
requirement that you win by two; no game can be decided by
only one point, no set by a single game. Thus a score of 40–40 is
referred to as "deuce." Whoever wins the next point gets an
"ad" or "advantage." If Rod Laver is serving, say, and he gains
this advantage, the score is announced either as "advantage,
Laver," or, less formally, "ad-in." ("Ad-out" is when the receiver
holds the advantage.) If the same player also wins the following point, he's two up, which gives him the game. But if he
loses that second one, his advantage is canceled and the score
reverts to deuce. Theoretically, a match could last all day or all
night, and actually there have been some that have. In the Indoor Championships in 1968, Mark Cox and Bobby Wilson, a
doubles team from England, were pitted against two American
players, Charlie Pasarell and Ron Holmberg. The Englishmen
eventually won the affair by 26–24, 17–19, 30–28. That's a total
of 144 games, many of which went to deuce several times. They
finished at two o'clock in the morning after playing for more
than six hours. And, mind you, that match was only two out of

three. Imagine how long they might have been playing if the match had been three out of five.

Especially in weekend competition, where somebody else is probably waiting for the court—and where playing that long might invite a heart attack—these marathon matches are silly. We badly need a better scoring system. Dozens have been tested over the years, of course, and I've personally tried almost all of them. Each one seemed to have its own drawbacks. So finally I devised a scoring system of my own—essentially a refinement of traditional rules rather than a radical departure from them—which I hereby give its public unveiling: The Talbert Scoring System.

My system dispenses with the usual requirement that you win by two or more. Winning by one is enough. When the game reaches deuce, the next point decides it. Whoever wins six games first takes the set—regardless of whether the other guy has five. The only exception is the final set, if the score going into it is tied. Then that set must be won by sudden death. Eight points are played, alternating serves. The player winning five points wins. If it's tied at four points each, a player then must win two points in a row to capture the match.

The customary argument against such a plan is that the server of the first game has an unfair advantage; he can win the set by simply holding service. This is the reason why traditional rules require a margin of at least two games; you have to break service to win. But early in the match, this doesn't bother me. After all, the advantage alternates. If I lose the first set on serve 6–5, I serve first in the next one, and now the advantage is mine, you see; *I* can win the set by holding service. Let's say two opponents are evenly matched, and through twenty-two games they both hold service. By traditional scoring, they'd still be in the first set, tied at 11–11. They'd also be tied by the Talbert system, but now they'd be entering the *third* set. They each won a previous set, 6–5. And the last set, I contend, is where the excitement lies in tennis—in fact, the best action is near the end in *any* sporting event when there's well-matched competition. Football, basketball, horse racing, tennis—they're the same in this respect. And with my system, you reach this exciting part more quickly; there's no three-hour delay before the climax. At five games all, sudden death takes over.

A variation of my system has been labeled the "pro set" because the professionals often use it. Again, the next point after deuce decides the game, and a set can be won by six games to five—even, in this case, the rubber set. The difference is that when any set reaches 5–5, it's decided by a 9-point tie-break. In a tie-break, the serve changes hands. Let's say I'm playing Rod Laver in a tie-break. (For some reason, I keep imagining myself playing against Laver.) Laver wins the spin and elects to serve first. He delivers his first serve into the right-hand court, his second one into the left. Then I serve two in the same sequence. The pattern is repeated until someone wins five points. If the points are even at 4–4, Laver has his choice of serving the ninth, deciding point into either the left court or the right. In a doubles match, Laver would serve the first and second points, his partner the fifth and sixth. Similarly, I would serve points three and four, and *my* partner points seven, eight, and nine. This system is also called VASSS "no-ad." Those initials stand for Van Alen Simplified Scoring System, James Van Alen being the man who thought it up.

Another of Van Alen's scoring innovations, with much to recommend it for weekend play, is one he calls "31-Point." Serving is the same as in table tennis. Each player serves five consecutive points, the first to the right court, the second to the left, then right, left, right again; you always begin with the right. The first player to score 31 points is the winner, *except* when the score becomes tied at 30–30, in which case the players alternate service until someone gets two points ahead.

Among the many assets of 31-Point is that you can tell with

remarkable accuracy how long it will take to play. A full set, for which the score would be 31–29, runs about twenty-five minutes; a two-set match can be completed in an hour (with a nine-point tie-break to decide the winner if each player takes one set). Two full sets under the Talbert scoring system would run perhaps a quarter hour longer. Using the traditional scoring system, a set could be 6–0 or 20–18, say; you never know *when* it might end. Obviously, this complicates scheduling.

When players of unequal ability meet, 31-Point has the added advantage of being suitable for establishing handicaps. As in golf, a good player who shoots scratch (no handicap) can be evenly matched against a lesser opponent by giving the second guy a head start—the range being anywhere from one point to thirty, depending on the difference in their skills. Of course, traditionally-scored sets can be handicapped too—staking one player to a 2–0 lead in games, say, or granting a slight underdog one "gimmee point" per set, which he can take at his discretion to win a critical point—but to do so is usually awkward; there's none of the refinement or the ease of comprehension that 31-Point provides.

Various other methods for handicapping matches have nothing to do with the scoring system. Some of them, for that matter —the more bizarre techniques—have little to do with tennis. But it's fun to try to even things up by handicapping, and you can try any device that seems likely.

A good one, if your opponent has limited skills, is to play strictly defense against him—without telling him so, if you wish. Sometimes that makes it better. This is a player you could beat rather handily, so you decide *not* to beat him but to make him beat himself. Resisting all temptations to mount an attack— no difficult serves, no placements, no smashes—you concentrate wholly on just hitting the ball back to him until he finally beats himself by making errors.

Sometimes one player keeps defeating another on the strength of a monstrous serve; otherwise, their skills are much alike. To defuse that big weapon and make their rivalry closer, you could restrict the big server to only one try—making a single fault the same as a double fault for him—or have him serve from a yard or so behind the base line. Or from three yards behind it, or five, or ten, or back on the steps of the clubhouse, if need be, to even the competition.

A superior player who wants some good exercise might challenge a team of two lesser opponents or, in singles, let the other guy include the alleys in his target so he's hitting to a full doubles court.

A *reasonably* good contest can often be created with appropriate handicaps. But on other occasions the difference in skills is simply too large to bridge. Attempts to make things even are absolute nonsense—which doesn't mean they can't provide some laughs.

If you want to see some wild ones, go to Hollywood, California. A good many movie stars enjoy playing tennis, especially against top-ranking players. What they want to do, of course, is beat them. Why not? Everyone wants to knock off the champs. Then at the studio or some fancy cocktail party they could announce, very casually, "Played Gonzales today at tennis. Yeah, the national champion. Managed to beat him too." Many top-ranked players, including myself, were delighted to give them the chance. I'd never want to *live* in Hollywood, you understand, but it's not a bad place to visit—sunshine, pretty girls, a groovy scene. Anyhow, I remember one summer afternoon when a number of not-terribly-good Hollywood players decided they were going to beat Bobby Riggs. It would be futile, of course, to try to handicap the score; Bobby, if he had to, could have shut them out stone cold. So they thought up some other devices. One trick was to make him wear a raincoat while playing. The weather was sunny, about 90 degrees, but the gimmick didn't work. Then they added hip boots, but that was no better. At one stage, they prevailed on a studio prop man to dig up a pair of snowshoes. Then they put some chairs and a bench on the court to surround Riggs with an obstacle course. Later, they tied one arm behind his back. Bobby just smiled and kept hitting the ball back, maybe picking up a buck or two on side bets.

The only way I know of you might beat a man that good is in a game called Drink-or-Sniff. You use the traditional scoring system, and at the end of each game the victorious player takes a one-ounce drink from a bottle kept handy primarily for medicinal purposes; the loser gets only a sniff. Well, figure it out mathematically. A player must win a minimum of six games to take a set, twelve to win a best-of-three match. By the time your opponent gets close to match point—even if his name is Rod Laver or Don Budge—you conceivably could win a game or two against him.

Chapter 14

WEEKEND TOURNAMENTS

LET'S IMAGINE ourselves the directors of a weekend tennis tournament involving the five top-rated players in the United States plus an equal number of celebrity players invited to stimulate interest. We've decided on ten because that's all we can accommodate with our limited number of courts and just one weekend.

On the morning we issued our invitations, the five top players, in order of their ranking, were (1) Arthur Ashe; (2) Clark Graebner; (3) Stan Smith; (4) Cliff Richey, and (5) Bob Lutz.

Each of them accepted, as did the following celebrities, listed in no special order: Robert McNamara, former Secretary of Defense (chosen for the tournament because of his skill as a tactician); Kirk Douglas, the actor (as a favor to the ladies); Peter Ustinov (for his unique serve and after-dinner stories); Hank Greenberg (as a convert from another field of sport); and Sargent Shriver, our former ambassador to France (as a representative of the Diplomatic Corps).

Each of these celebrities is a pretty good player, but obviously no match for the top five. We're confronted with our first big decision. Should we, in effect, hold two separate tournaments—an "A" bracket for the stars, a "B" for the others—or mix them up and impose some sort of handicap? The traditional choice would be the former, of course. In most major tournaments, any assumed advantage is sufficient cause for strict segregation. A boy aged sixteen, say, will seldom play one eighteen; they'll compete in different classes.

But ours is a more informal affair, dedicated to the proposition of having some fun, so let's have them all intermingle. We'll announce a simple ground rule to help even things up: Anyone in the top five, when he plays a celebrity (members of the top five are themselves only semi-celebrities, or celebrities only in tennis circles), must spot him a 3–0 lead in games each set. It won't be enough, but the stars will play along with it, adopting what we sometimes call "the customer's game" to give the *appearance* that they're evenly matched. The stars enjoy a little fun too.

That much decided, we face another choice: whether to have an elimination tournament or round robin. Let's make up charts for both of them, then compare their advantages and drawbacks.

Most big tournaments are single eliminations. Losing any match puts you out of contention. The winner must defeat a succession of opponents, but he doesn't have to play each contestant. The U. S. Open championships, held at Forest Hills, illustrate how it works. The original field accommodates 128 players. They pair off in the first round and half of them lose; now there are 64 left. (The first-round losers in elimination tournaments often compete in a separate loser's bracket—simply so they don't have to go home after one match. At Wimbledon, this loser's bracket is called "The Plate.") The second round reduces the field to 32; the third round cuts it to 16. In "the round of 16," tension starts to mount, and with each succeeding round it gets tighter—in the quarter finals, which begin with 8 players and knock out 4; the semifinals, in which the number goes down to 2; and then the climactic confrontation of survivors to determine which one gets the trophy.

It's a fine, efficient way to decide a major title, but a friendly weekend tournament is different. The first thing we notice when we start to rough our chart up is that we have an inconvenient number of players. Instead of 8 or 16, we have 10. This means our chart will have "byes." To determine the number of

byes on the chart, we subtract the number of players we have
from the next higher power of two. (The powers of two being
2, 4, 8, 16, 32, 64, 128, and so on.) In our case, 16 is next
higher after 10. We therefore subtract 10 from 16 and get 6. Six
of our players will have first-round byes. Which means that less
than half of them will play in that round. Notice that the only
reason for having byes is to bring into the second round a number of players that is a power of two; it is *not* to protect a player
from losing early. Since our chart, as it happens, will have an
even number of byes—6—we'll put half of them on the top of
the draw (on the even numbers beginning with 2, the rules say)
and half on the bottom (on the odd numbers beginning with the
last odd number). In cases where the number of byes is uneven,
the extra one goes on the bottom. Translated into a chart, it
looks like this:

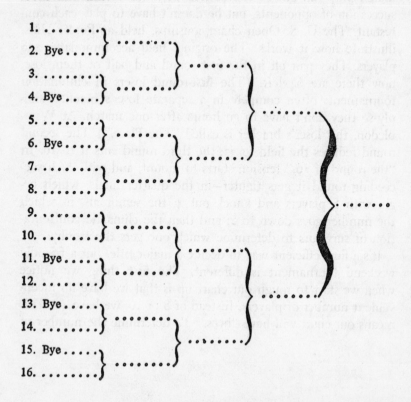

1. . . . .

2. Bye . . . . .

3. . . . .

4. Bye . . . . .

5. . . . .

6. Bye . . . . .

7. . . . .

8. . . . .

9. . . . .

10. . . . .

11. Bye . . . . .

12. . . . .

13. Bye . . . . .

14. . . . .

15. Bye . . . . .

16. . . . .

The next step, obviously, is to fill in the names, and the fairest way to do it is by lot. Just pull them out of a hat. USLTA Tournament Regulations say, "The byes in the top half shall be the names drawn first. The next names drawn shall be placed in the first round. The byes in the bottom half are drawn last."

Okay, so we put all ten names in a hat and have somebody draw them out, one by one. The first three selected are Graebner, Ashe, and Shriver. They get first-round byes at the top of the chart, in positions one, three, and five respectively. Next out come Ustinov, Richey, Douglas, and Greenberg. Those four are listed for first-round matches, in positions seven, eight, nine, and ten. Then the names McNamara, Lutz, and Smith are drawn. These three get lower-half byes. Our chart is now complete:

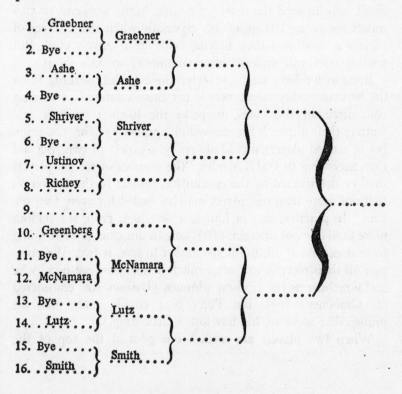

The trouble with this draw, from our standpoint of tournament directors, is that its structure is anticlimactic. The two top players, Ashe and Graebner, are scheduled to meet too early —in the very first match they play. Ustinov against Richey opens the tournament, then Douglas faces Greenberg. (Actually, these two matches could be played simultaneously, assuming we have the use of two courts.) Then we go to the top of the chart and begin the second round: Graebner versus Ashe. The interest of many spectators will lag after this match; they'll assume that the winner is going on to take the trophy. How much better it would be if the draw were contructed so that Ashe could meet Graebner in the finals. Then tension would build as they moved toward each other through each succeeding round—barring any upsets, of course.

So let's make a new draw, and this time we'll "seed" it. We don't *have* to seed the draw, of course. Many weekend tournaments are better left unseeded, especially when the number of players is small and their playing skills are relatively even. But seeding ours will make it more dramatic, so let's do it.

Byes, as we have seen, are determined by lot. Seeding is on the basis of ability. Some people get them confused. A seeding committee—in this case, us—picks the likeliest winners and scatters them through the draw. For simplicity's sake, the number of seeded players should always be a power of two. Beyond that, according to USLTA rules, "the number of seeded players shall be determined by the committee, subject to the limitation that not more than one player may be seeded for every four entries." In practice, one in four is a very high ratio; it's seldom more than one out of eight, often less. In our case, if we're going to seed anyone at all, the best number to seed is two. We compare all their records, and after much deliberation we pick Ashe and Graebner as the likeliest winners. (Ustinov was considered for Graebner's spot, but Peter is a couple years past his prime; that serve of his has lost a little zing.)

When two players are seeded, one goes at the top of the

upper half of the draw, the other at the bottom of the lower half; which one goes where is determined by lot. So we put the names in a hat and draw one out: Graebner. Graebner goes at the top of the draw, Ashe at the bottom; they can meet each other only in the finals. (If we were seeding four players, the third and fourth seeds would go at the top of the second quarter of the draw and at the bottom of the third quarter, with those positions again decided by lot.) Now we fill the chart out the same way as before—by pulling the other names from the hat one by one and listing them in that order down the chart where there are openings. Let's say we draw them in this sequence: Greenberg, Ustinov, Shriver, Lutz, Douglas, Richey, McNamara, Smith. Our completed chart looks like this:

It might be fun to imagine how our tournament would go. Maybe it would be something like this:

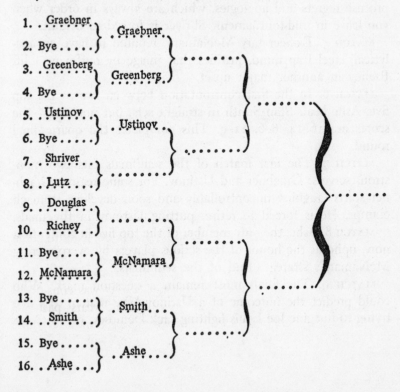

1. Graebner
2. Bye
3. Greenberg
4. Bye
5. Ustinov
6. Bye
7. Shriver
8. Lutz
9. Douglas
10. Richey
11. Bye
12. McNamara
13. Bye
14. Smith
15. Bye
16. Ashe

Graebner
Greenberg
Ustinov
McNamara
Smith
Ashe

MATCH 1. The inevitable upset that spices every tournament occurs right off the bat when Sargent Shriver beats Bob Lutz. Lutz appeared tired; he had to drive all night to get here. Now he can start driving back again, because one loss puts you out of contention.

MATCH 2. Kirk Douglas struggles heroically in the true Hollywood tradition, but Cliff Richey, the pride of San Angelo, Texas, prevails in five exciting sets.

MATCH 3. In a battle of sluggers, Hank Greenberg holds his own through the first two sets, but Henry is eventually betrayed by his years, and Graebner wins going away.

MATCH 4. Enormously confident after his upset of Lutz, Sargent Shriver leads Peter Ustinov 5–0 in the first set when a message arrives telling him of an unexpected political development that requires his immediate departure for Paris. Amid profuse regrets and apologies, which are always in order when you leave in mid-tournament, Shriver is forced to default.

MATCH 5. Ex-Secretary McNamara, reputed to have an analytical, steel trap mind, justifies that image by outfoxing Cliff Richey in another major upset.

MATCH 6. In the first confrontation between two of the top five, Ashe beats Stan Smith in straight sets, but not easily—the scores are 16–14, 8–6, 11–9. This completes the quarter-final round.

MATCH 7. The first match of the semifinals pits two monstrous servers: Graebner and Ustinov. For some reason, Graebner starts laughing uncontrollably and soon develops stomach cramps. He is forced to retire, putting Ustinov in the finals.

MATCH 8. Ashe, the only member of the top five in contention now, upholds the honor of the serious players by overpowering McNamara's strategy. End of the semifinals.

MATCH 9. The finals must remain a question mark. Who could predict the outcome of a Ustinov-Ashe match? It's like trying to imagine Joe Louis fighting Jack Dempsey, or Ty Cobb batting against Sandy Koufax. Your guess is probably as good as mine as to what would likely happen.

Now let's examine our finished chart:

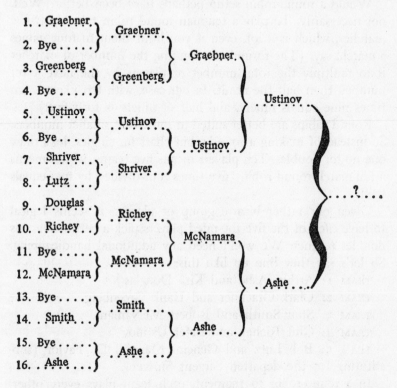

1. Graebner
2. Bye ...... } Graebner
3. Greenberg } Graebner
4. Bye ...... } Greenberg
5. Ustinov } Ustinov
6. Bye ...... } Ustinov
7. Shriver } Ustinov
8. Lutz ...... } Shriver
9. Douglas } ? ......
10. Richey ...... } Richey
11. Bye ...... } McNamara
12. McNamara } McNamara
13. Bye ...... } Smith
14. Smith ...... } Ashe
15. Bye ...... } Ashe ......
16. Ashe ...... } Ashe

The first thing we notice is the efficiency of this setup. In an elimination tournament, the field is reduced quickly. Determining the winner took only nine matches. Some players played three times, but others played just once, and for the latter perhaps the end came *too* quickly. Most participants in a casual weekend tournament want the assurance of a little more action.

We also observe that, in spite of our seeding, Graebner and Ashe never met. For that matter, neither did Greenberg and

Ustinov (what a battle of the titans *that* would have been),
or Smith and Lutz, or Douglas and Shriver—in fact, out of a
possible forty-five pairings, only nine were actually realized.

Would a round-robin setup perhaps have been better? Well,
not necessarily. To play a ten-man round robin takes forty-five
matches, which is a lot, even if you limit them to four games
a match, say. (The formula for figuring the number of matches
is to multiply the total number of players by the next lower
number, then half the result. In our case, with ten players, ten
times nine equals ninety, and half of ninety is forty-five.)

Round robins are better suited to somewhat smaller numbers.
So instead of making a round-robin chart for singles, let's draw
one up for doubles. Ten players means five teams, which means
a ten-match round robin (five times four divided by two equals
ten).

Given our rather bizarre group of players, it seems logical
to have each of the five top-rated players pick a celebrity as his
doubles partner. We won't need any additional handicapping.
So let's say they line up like this:

TEAM 1: Arthur Ashe and Kirk Douglas

TEAM 2: Clark Graebner and Hank Greenberg

TEAM 3: Stan Smith and Robert McNamara

TEAM 4: Cliff Richey and Peter Ustinov

TEAM 5: Bob Lutz and General Maxwell D. Taylor (sub-
stituting for the departed Sargent Shriver).

In a round-robin tournament, each team plays every other.
There are no worries about byes or seeding. Each match can be
as long as we want it to be, depending on how many courts
we have and how much time is available. Since we used the
traditional scoring system for singles, let's use the VASSS 31-
Point for doubles. And just to make it interesting, let's com-
plicate things a bit. Let's say the winning team in each match
gets a five-point bonus for winning, plus a number of points
equal to its margin of victory, in addition to the 31 it scores.

The Ashe-Douglas team defeats Graebner-Greenberg by 31–25. The losers get only the twenty-five points they scored; the winners get forty-two (the thirty-one they scored, plus five for winning, plus six, their margin of victory). This encourages each team to bear down throughout the tournament, giving them an incentive to win, and win big. The team with the highest total of points at the end is the one that gets the trophies.

Here's what the score sheet might look like at the beginning:

TEAMS TO PLAY	SCORE	POINTS				
		1	2	3	4	5
Ashe-Douglas vs. Graebner-Greenberg (Team 1) (Team 2)						
Smith-McNamara vs. Richey-Ustinov (Team 3) (Team 4)						
Lutz-Taylor vs. Ashe-Douglas (Team 5) (Team 1)						
Graebner-Greenberg vs. Smith-McNamara (Team 2) (Team 3)						
Richey-Ustinov vs. Lutz-Taylor (Team 4) (Team 5)						
Ashe-Douglas vs. Smith-McNamara (Team 1) (Team 3)						
Graebner-Greenberg vs. Richey-Ustinov (Team 2) (Team 4)						
Smith-McNamara vs. Lutz-Taylor (Team 3) (Team 5)						
Richey-Ustinov vs. Ashe-Douglas (Team 4) (Team 1)						
Lutz-Taylor vs. Graebner-Greenberg (Team 5) (Team 2)						
TOTAL POINTS						

And at the end:

TEAMS TO PLAY	SCORE	POINTS				
		1	2	3	4	5
Ashe-Douglas vs. Graebner-Greenberg (Team 1) (Team 2)	31-25	42	25			
Smith-McNamara vs. Richey-Ustinov (Team 3) (Team 4)	27-31			27	40	
Lutz-Taylor vs. Ashe-Douglas (Team 5) (Team 1)	31-24	24				43
Graebner-Greenberg vs. Smith-McNamara (Team 2) (Team 3)	31-28		37	28		
Richey-Ustinov vs. Lutz-Taylor (Team 4) (Team 5)	26-31				26	41
Ashe-Douglas vs. Smith-McNamara (Team 1) (Team 3)	29-31	29		38		
Graebner-Greenberg vs. Richey-Ustinov (Team 2) (Team 4)	31-21		46		21	
Smith-McNamara vs. Lutz-Taylor (Team 3) (Team 5)	19-31			19		48
Richey-Ustinov vs. Ashe-Douglas (Team 4) (Team 1)	22-31	45			22	
Lutz-Taylor vs. Graebner-Greenberg (Team 5) (Team 2)	24-31		43			24
TOTAL POINTS		140	153	112	109	156

You'll notice that two teams lost only one match—Graebner-Greenberg (Team 2) and Lutz-Taylor (Team 5). If we were scoring on the basis of wins and losses, these two would meet again in a play-off. Another acceptable scoring system is simply to total the points scored by each team, without adding bonus points. If we had chosen this system, we would have a different winner: the Graebner-Greenberg partnership scored 118 points, one more than the Lutz-Taylor team. But the Lutz-Taylor team permitted their opponents fewer points, which accounts for their victory by our system. By chance, the final match pitted these teams against each other. It was much more exciting than the score might suggest, because by this stage, the trophy was more important than the match. The Lutz-Taylor team could wrap up the trophy by scoring at least 23 points. So the Graebner-Greenberg partnership, while winning the match, simultaneously lost the tournament by allowing their opponents one more point than they needed.

Round-robin tournaments are always lots of fun, regardless of what scoring system you use, because everyone gets a chance to play everyone else. It's the ideal social mixer. We can be pleased with the weekend combination we planned—an elimination draw for the singles competition, then a ten-match round robin for the doubles.

Of course, drawing up the plans for a real weekend tournament would just be the start of our duties. The directors of a tournament and the referee (who presides over the doings in an off-court capacity, not in the manner of a football referee, whose function is served in tennis by the umpire) have a hard, many-faceted job. They must schedule the matches, line up officials, arrange for the feeding and housing of the players, and cope with a thousand diverse responsibilities that keep them hopping every minute. But they are *not* required to put up with outrageous behavior on the part of unco-operative players.

I've known tennis players to conduct themselves so abominably at a tournament that they brought about its permanent cancellation. Others are such boors that they spoil all the fun. So numerous are the breaches of good manners I've observed that I'm moved to draw up a list of rules for participants. You can call them the ten commandments of tennis tournaments.

I. *Thou shalt not indulge in constant complaints.* "The draw is unfair." "The courts are poorly surfaced." "The weather is lousy." "The facilities are awful." "The linesmen should be provided with seeing-eye dogs." "The only thing I've done here is wait, wait, wait." Such comments do nothing to make a tournament more pleasant. The directors are undoubtedly trying their best, and if your first match pits you against the number one seed, well, next time perhaps your luck will be better.

II. *Thou shalt not expect the tournament to be tailored to thy personal convenience.* Whatever your schedule of matches is, accept it. Even if you happen to be the top-seeded player, don't be a prima donna. Don't balk at playing an early morning match, say, just because you like to sleep late. Don't pull an Henri Cochet, in other words. When Cochet was a French star, in the 1940s, he was invited by Perry T. Jones, the developer of so many top California players, to travel to Los Angeles for the Pacific South-West tournament. In those days it was considered uncivilized in France to exercise any earlier than midafternoon, and Cochet was adamant when Jones told him the first morning that he was scheduled to play at eleven o'clock. "I never play before two," Cochet replied firmly. It was already eleven, so Jones had little choice if he wanted to keep his top star in the tournament. He turned to the young man who was to be Cochet's opponent and said, "Right, you're scratched—bad behavior." And all Cochet's matches for the rest of the week were scheduled for late afternoon.

I've benefited from enough preferential treatment myself to know how other players resent it. Dick Savitt and I used to plead—legitimately, I might add—that the pressure of business denied us the opportunity of participating in this-or-that week-long tournament but we'd like to play if we could arrive a little late. "Could we come on Thursday?" we frequently suggested. And more often than not, since we were "famous-name players," the draw would be arranged so we could pull in three days late, play two matches against rabbits in one afternoon to catch up, and sweep elegantly into the finals on Sunday. I didn't blame the other guys one bit for despising us.

III. *Thou shalt not scream and holler if a mistake has been made*. Let's say your name was omitted from the draw. Or maybe you're scheduled for two matches at once. There's no need to wail as if you were mortally wounded. Somewhere nearby is the tournament referee. One of his functions is to deal with such matters. Present your problem calmly and he'll calmly resolve it. Most tournaments are hectic enough already without exaggerated lamentations.

IV. *Thou shalt not overstay thy welcome.* House guests are expected to depart from a tournament as soon as it ends or as soon as they're eliminated, whichever event comes first. Nor should they appear two days in advance. Players have been known to stretch the weekend both ways—arriving on a Thursday morning perhaps, then staying until the following Wednesday afternoon—and travel directly from one tournament to another as long as they keep getting asked. I've known a few who hung around three or four weeks, until the next invitation showed up. It's a very pleasant life. It's called freeloading.

V. *Thou shalt not disregard the clock.* If you're scheduled for a match at 9:00 A.M., be there by 8:45. If lunch is served at one o'clock, don't show up at two. Most tournament weekends are run on tight schedules. Carefully study the timetable, then follow it.

VI. *Thou shalt not appear for a match in no condition to play it.* Do your celebrating *after* you compete, not before. And try not to schedule your commitments so tight that one is the same as the other. The trouble with being on the circuit all summer was that the tournaments invariably came too close together; there was no chance in between them to unwind. I remember one year when Don McNeill was national champion and the two of us had competed in a tournament in Louisville. The closing night party was still swinging at dawn, but we had to pull ourselves away and set out for Indianapolis, where another tournament began that afternoon. McNeill had won at Louisville, so I volunteered to drive while Don continued to celebrate his victory. When we reached Indianapolis, where McNeill was the top seed, he was hardly in the ideal condition for playing tennis. His opening round opponent started tearing him to shreds; the first set was over in ten minutes, 6–0. Panicked by the realization that another set like that would eliminate his top seed in the opening round, the tournament director got a sudden inspiration. He glanced at the sky and called the match because of darkness. It was an embarrassing position for Don to have put him in, because the time was only six o'clock and it was the middle of June; there was a good three hours of daylight remaining. The following morning, a contrite McNeill redeemed himself by winning the next two sets, 6–0, 6–1.

VII. *Thou shalt not be resentful of alien players.* Even at Forest Hills, believe it or not, there are regular players who oppose the "intrusions" of people like Arthur Ashe or Rod Laver. They would rather keep the courts all to themselves. Similarly, there are always a couple players on the circuit who barge into country clubs and chase the members off the courts, as if they had no business being there. It saddens me to see these narrow attitudes expressed. Members and guests should enjoy each other's company, whether it's at Forest Hills or a weekend retreat.

VIII. *Thou shalt not make gratuitous disparaging remarks.* I remember as if it had been yesterday the banquet at the close of a weekend tennis tournament in never mind what midwestern city. As is customary, a few of us who were visiting from out of town got up to say how much we'd enjoyed it. His name doesn't matter, but one player, when his turn came, rose, looked around with obvious distaste, and began his remarks like this: "Well, I've seen some ugly broads in my time, but the dames in this hick town take the prize." And that was just for openers. In the next few minutes, he insulted everyone present and heaped contempt on the entire community. I believe it was the only occasion in my life when I've ever been ashamed of being a tennis player. The fact that he'd been drinking was an inadequate excuse. There *is* no excuse for behavior like that. When you're a guest, it behooves you to act like one, not like an ill-mannered brat. The hosts on this occasion were so stunned, so distraught, that the tournament was never held again.

IX. *Thou shalt not miss opportunities to be of some assistance.* Tournament hosts need all the help they can get. They have too few linesmen. They lack a good scorekeeper. When a mother and father are out on the court, someone must keep their young children entertained. There are a hundred different ways in which a guest can be useful if he only looks around with that in mind.

X. *Thou shalt not take advantage of thy host.* I remember one player, a guy from California, who called home twice a day from Newport, Rhode Island, and charged it to his hostess' phone bill. Another always drank his host's liquor cabinet dry, practically ate him out of house and home, and asked the man's wife to do his washing and ironing. Visiting players often commandeer the family car or expect their host to keep them constantly entertained. But these tricks are fairly routine. Probably the most ingenious I ever ran across was the happy birthday caper. Let's say the player's name was Joe. His charm and good manners so endeared him to hosts that they vied for his company in every city on the circuit. Once when Joe's birthday fell on a tournament weekend, his host of the moment threw a lavish party for him and showered him with expensive gifts. Joe was quick to recognize a good thing when he saw it, and he casually let drop at each subsequent tournament that it happened to be his birthday. In his prime, he had fifty-two birthdays a year. I tell you, you meet some dandies playing tennis.

Chapter 15

PUTTING IT ALL TOGETHER

ON A GRAY, rainy Saturday afternoon last September, in a semi-finals match of the U. S. Open championships, Rod Laver, the top-seeded Australian star, met Arthur Ashe, the last American in contention. As I watched them warming up on the center court at Forest Hills, where the memories of so many great moments fill the air, I fully expected Laver to win. He's unquestionably the top player in the world right now, and to my mind one of the five or six best of all time—the others being Tilden, Budge, Kramer, and Gonzales, with maybe Bobby Riggs in there too. I like Rod personally, but I was pulling for Ashe. After facing the Australians in so many Davis Cup matches, I think of them automatically as our arch rivals in tennis, and I wanted to see an American win.

Arthur won the toss and elected to receive. It's the same choice I would have made. Weekenders in the audience were possibly surprised—most of them are convinced it's always best to serve first—but Ashe had done his homework, he'd studied his opponent (which too few weekend players do), and he knew that Laver often warms up slowly. If you catch him cold and break him in the very first game, you're off to a flying start. At four-thirty, under threatening skies, the match got under way. In the first game, Laver held service at love. So much for *that* piece of strategy.

"Game to Laver," the umpire announced. "Laver leads, one game to love."

Arthur came back to hold *his* serve at love, then continued to play as well as I have ever seen him play, but Laver possesses truly phenomenal talent and he simply had Arthur outclassed. It was evident right from the start. Ashe would struggle valiantly, and for a while might even lead (Laver quite frequently loses the first set, then sweeps the next three with comparative ease, as if unconsciously handicapping the match to make it interesting), but the trained eye saw at once which man would win.

Nonetheless, I thought Laver looked vulnerable that day. His game lacked its usual consistency. He was playing well, knocking off an assortment of brilliant winners, but he was making more mistakes than is his custom—four faulted serves in the first game, for example. It was doubtless due in part to the great pressure he was under. Rod was on the threshold of his second Grand Slam, a feat that had never been accomplished before; a victory in this tournament would complete it. Besides that distinction, there was a large purse at stake—$16,000 for the winner—and Laver appreciates money. He was also on a winning streak of twenty-eight straight matches that extended over a period of three months. The tension that had been gradually mounting all that time was beginning to affect his tennis, I felt. Against Ashe, he seemed a bit overanxious. I thought the right player might have beaten him.

Unfortunately, Ashe was ill-suited to the job because he plays the kind of game that Laver thrives on—the all-out "big" game, slam-bang, go-for-broke. Laver can play it too, and play it better. He isn't a very big guy—just 5'8" or so, no more than 145 pounds—but he has great wrists and he hits the ball *hard*. They don't call him the Rocket for nothing. When you try to slug it out with Laver, you wind up on the canvas. No, it would take someone with a different style entirely, a steadier player with more finesse and greater patience, someone who could exploit Laver's present frame of mind. I found myself wishing I were twenty-five years younger and out there on the center court myself.

"Game to Laver," the umpire announced. "Laver leads, four games to two, first set."

He had broken Ashe's service with a beautiful backhand crosscourt, and applause was rolling down from the crowd. Twenty-five years ago, that applause had been for me. I was the front-runner in this tournament then. My opponent in the semifinals was Pancho Segura. He carried me to five sets before I beat him. It was a good match, an exciting match, and the spectators had enjoyed it, just as they were enjoying it now. Twenty-five years ago, but it might have been just yesterday. Nothing seems to have changed here. The courts had looked exactly the same on that occasion. The clubhouse and the stadium were no different, then and now. It seemed, on this overcast, ghostly afternoon, as if time had stood still at Forest Hills.

"Game to Ashe," the umpire was saying. "Laver leads, four games to three."

Good boy, Arthur. He had broken Laver back. That strengthened my suspicion that Rod's game was slightly shaky. Usually, when he's ahead, he doesn't let you off the hook. Dammit, he *could* be beaten today. I wondered whether I could have done it.

Watching him even more carefully now, I began to plan my strategy against him. Laver is a left-handed player, of course, but his backhand is even more formidable than his forehand, so I can regard him as I would the average right-handed player: slightly stronger to his right than to his left. A right-hander's reach in that direction is much greater, though. Laver has to reach across his body. So when I'm serving to the right court, I'll serve to Rod's backhand and give him a lot of wide, sweeping slices; they tend to draw southpaws off the court. In the left

PUTTING IT ALL TOGETHER 205

court, I'll serve straight at him rather than away from him. He likes to hit from the outside, so I'll jam him. I'll try to play the majority of my shots down the middle instead of hitting wide to either his backhand or his forehand. I'll use the defensive lob if he tries to move in. The big thing is to keep him from advancing to the net. If I let him take the net, he's going to kill me. I'll have to hit deep, keep forcing him back, don't give him anything easy to attack. Be consistent, be lucky, and hit exactly the right shot to exactly the right place— that's the only way to beat Laver.

On the court now, chasing one of Ashe's looping forehands, Laver slipped and the ball got safely past him. The rain had been falling off and on for a week, and the grass had become torn up and soggy. Earlier in the tournament, I'd noticed Laver wearing spikes. Then he'd changed to sneakers, then back to spikes again, and now he'd returned to sneakers. Apparently the footing was bothering Rod, regardless of which shoes he had on. I filed the information away in my mind, wondering what effect a sequence of lobs and dinks might have.

By this time, Ashe had temporarily pulled ahead. After holding his own service he had broken Laver again—the second service break in three games. It was at this point that reality and imagination diverged. Ashe was no longer out there on the court representing America's last hope in this tournament. In my mind, I had taken his place.

"Game to Talbert," the umpire announced. "Talbert leads, five games to four."

With that one-break advantage I'd inherited from Arthur, I held service to run out the first set, 6–4.

So there I was on the center court at Forest Hills again, where I had wanted to be for so much of my life—ever since my father came home from work one day and put a bulky, odd-shaped package in my hands: my first tennis racket and a single white ball. It took many, many thousands of hours of practice to realize the dream that began that afternoon. And all those difficult seasons on the circuit when I worried that I might never be good enough. And the hundreds of people who helped along the way—older and better players who gave me tips and encouragement; tournament officials who found a place for me in the draw; dozens of generous patrons of the game who opened their homes to a young, struggling player with seldom enough money for hotel rooms. The debt I felt I owed them could only be repaid by reaching Forest Hills someday and playing for the national championship. When I finally succeeded, I sensed them there beside me, ready to help again if I should need them.

"Concentrate, boy. You got to *concentrate* in tennis. You'll never get to Forest Hills daydreaming." I recognized the voice as that of Roy Fitzgerald, my first instructor, when I was playing on the public courts in Cincinnati. I hadn't seen Roy for, oh, I don't know how long. But his advice had stuck with me, and I *did* have to concentrate. Laver was preparing to serve.

Toss. Crunch. Ace.

"Fifteen-love," said the umpire.

Toss. Crunch. Ace.

"Thirty-love."

What is this, a daydream or a nightmare, I wondered.

Toss. Crunch . . . Well, at least I got my racket on it that time.

"Forty-love," the umpire announced.

Laver delivered the next one even faster than the first three. I didn't even bother to swing at it. How does such a little guy hit a tennis ball so *hard?*

"Game to Laver," the umpire said. "Laver leads, one game to love, second set."

Well, now it's my turn. Things might pick up.

I served to Rod's backhand—a wide, sweeping slice. His return went by so fast I barely saw it.

"Love-fifteen," the umpire said.

In the ad court, as planned, I served directly at him. The result was exactly the same.

"Love-thirty," the umpire said.

Again I tried a wide slice serve to his backhand. His down-the-line return kicked up chalk.

"Love-forty."

This was getting monotonous. I wondered if I'd be the first man in Forest Hills history to play a whole set without getting one point.

That fear ended when Laver netted his next shot, but he atoned for it on the following point, and I was broken.

"Game to Laver. Laver leads, two games to love."

The third game was the same story with somewhat more variety. Rod didn't rely entirely on his aces; he also rushed the net and drilled high-powered volleys past me. By the fourth game, in which he broke me for the second time running by detonating a succession of fantastic placements, incredible shots he really had no business even trying, I could see it would be a long afternoon. My opponent was a better player than I was.

I had never let that realization bother me, however, and I had no intention of doing so now. Many of my opponents have been technically my betters, especially in those first rocky years on the circuit, yet I often managed somehow to defeat them. Being cast as the underdog in those days proved a blessing. It instilled in me the feeling, which I have never gotten over, that I always had to play my very best. If I didn't mount a steady, smart, well-balanced game—"putting it all together," the sports announcers call it—my chances of winning were almost nonexistent. That isn't the same as pessimism or a defeatist frame of mind. It's closer to the opposite, in fact. I approached every match with the conviction that I *would* win, but I'd have to work hard and bear down. If my opponent surged ahead, I couldn't let it disconcert me. Every point I got, I'd have to fight for. Politicians call this attitude "running scared," I believe, though it doesn't really signify fear. What it means is that they recognize a dangerous challenge and see the need to wage an all-out campaign. Tennis players should always take the court with that same outlook. It protects them from overconfidence, encourages their best efforts, and toughens them psychologically against moments such as this one, when they appear to have no chance at all.

Laver was playing tennis like a Fourth-of-July star-burst—in a series of brilliant and spectacular explosions that had the audience gasping in awe. His performance was so stunning that I tucked my racket under my arm and joined the applause myself. After all, what else could I do? I'd seen these inspired moments in great players before, hot streaks when their game approaches absolute perfection, and I knew I was powerless to do anything about it. I might just as well relax and admire it, I thought (at the same time slacking off a bit in order to conserve my energy), and calmly wait it out, like a head cold. By the sixth game, the fireworks had sufficiently cooled off so that I surprised myself by managing to hold service. The second set was Laver's, 6–1.

I hoped Rod would attempt to prolong his tour de force because I felt it had just about burned itself out and that his flashier shots would soon begin to miss. But Laver sensed the same thing, and wasn't having any. For the third set, he abandoned his flamboyant attack and settled into a conservative cat-and-mouse game. Naturally, I was aware of his deliberate taunt. It was as if he were saying, "Okay, Talbert. I blew you off the court playing *my* kind of tennis, now I'm going to whip you playing *your* kind."

Particularly at the highest levels of the sport—but in weekend play, too, to a lesser degree—tennis is a contest of wills. When one player shatters his opponent's morale, or otherwise assumes psychological command—as Rod hoped to do now by challenging my strength—the match is as good as over. Laver is adept at this aspect of the game. One often hears his "mental toughness" praised. He never stoops to gamesmanship or superficial psyching (and attempting to psych *him* is a total waste of time), but he's relentless in his efforts to bend opponents to his will. For my part, I was determined to withstand him.

Technically, the third set was the best of the match—less dazzling and dramatic than others, perhaps, but we both played steady, intelligent tennis on nearly equal terms. We were moving the ball around well, mixing our shots, attacking at the right time, setting up placements, matching each other in a sound, cohesive contest that left little to choose from between us. The score went to five-all, six-all, seven-all, Laver holding service with relative ease (in a pinch, he could always cut loose with that rocket, which I still hadn't figured out a method for handling), while I managed to do the same, though with more difficulty; several times he carried me to deuce on my service before I wiggled away. The set was on service—no break for either player—for twenty-three consecutive games. Laver seemed content to have it seesaw indefinitely, figuring, no doubt, that I'd tire before he did, and for the rest of the match he'd have me at his mercy.

But then, while he was serving the twenty-fourth game, Laver's luck briefly turned sour. One of my shots hit a soft clump of grass—the wet court grew increasingly rough as we played—took an odd hop, and slid beneath his racket.

"Love-fifteen," said the umpire.

The tempo of the set had been so steady until now, the play flowing smoothly in a back-and-forth rhythm, that the effect had been almost hypnotic. By intruding on this constancy, the bad bounce startled Laver. It was like a glass of cold water thrown in his face to wake him up. For the first time in the match—and the last—he double-faulted.

"Love-thirty," the umpire said.

He faulted again, then, trying to play it safe, hit his second serve too shallow in the service court. My attacking return passed him at the net.

"Love-forty."

Suddenly, Rod found himself confronted with set point—triple set point, in fact. By losing any of the next three points, he'd drop the set. He gave no sign at all of being rattled. Laver is a very cool customer indeed, and, besides, he had that megaton serve in his arsenal. He'd been blowing it past me all afternoon, and he was hitting it even harder now than previously.

Toss. Crunch. Ace.

"Fifteen-forty," said the umpire.

Toss. Crunch. Ace.

"Thirty-forty."

The whole situation seemed depressingly familiar. Come on, Talbert, I told myself, he's making you look foolish.

I lunged at the next one, barely got my racket on it, and swatted it in sheer desperation. The ball hit the tape at the top of the net, hung there an instant as if making up its mind, then rolled over and fell on Laver's side. The third set was mine 13–11.

I half expected Rod to throw his racket in disgust. That's what many players would have done under the circumstances, but not the unperturbable Mr. Cool. He just smiled, put his sweater on, and headed toward the locker room for the ten-minute intermission. As he passed me, he said, "I'll get it back later."

When I'd showered and changed clothes, I sat down for a minute to take stock of how things were going. I realized I was getting very tired. That last set was a long one. It had taken a lot out of me. I was one up on Laver, but my chances of defeating him could be considered no better than even. The Australians are always so superbly conditioned that they can tear you apart in the stretch. I'd seen it happen time after time.

And Laver is a fanatic on keeping in shape, even by Aussie standards. I imagined him doing pushups during the rest break. If the match went five sets, I thought, I'd have little hope of winning. Talbert, I told myself as the fourth set began, you've got to beat this character right now.

Laver had other ideas. He came out firing those rockets again, broke me immediately, held his own service, then easily broke me once more. Trailing 3–0, I was forced to switch signals. I decided to junk the set. Trying to catch up from that far behind would drain every ounce of what strength I had left. If I failed —and the odds were stacked high that I would—I'd have nothing left at all to carry on with. So I ran out the set just going through the motions, trying to save energy, plotting ahead, reconciled to the most arduous assignment in tennis: playing a fifth set against Laver.

Both of my earlier suspicions proved correct. I *did* become exhausted before the fifth set was finished, and Laver *was* over-anxious that day. He'd given no indication of it for the past couple hours (which seemed to me, at this stage, closer to a year), but now, sensing blood as he saw me growing weaker, he allowed his killer instinct free reign. He stalked me ominously until the score reached three-all, and then he started swinging for the knockout.

The boxing ring analogy is an apt one, I think. Both sports pit one man against another in grueling combat, and at that moment I felt precisely like a battle-weary middleweight, knees sagging, mind groggy, backed against the ropes, instinctively pawing the air in self-defense, propped up by nothing but the habits I'd acquired in a lifetime of playing this silly game, desperately trying to make it to the bell.

Laver was missing with a lot of his shots now, but I'm certain he reasoned he could afford to take big risks because he still had his serve—his atom bomb—to fall back on. There was no *way* I could beat him without breaking his service, and so far I'd done it only a couple of times all afternoon—thanks to luck, a bad bounce and a netcord. I could hardly count on help like that again.

Instincts and reflexes were all I had left now, plus the memories of a few thousand matches over the years, and the voices that, in my dazed state on this ghostly afternoon, were ringing in my ears again. The voices belonged to people who had always been there when I needed them.

"Just keep getting the ball back, Willy." That's Gardnar Mulloy, my old doubles partner, talking. "Remember how we won all those tournaments together? Get the ball back—that was rule one. This guy's too eager. Let him make mistakes. Hang in there. You're doing all right."

All right, hell. Laver's mauling me.

Nevertheless, his explosions are misfiring often enough so that, incredibly, I'm still in contention. In fact, having served first, I'm officially ahead—five games to four, the scoreboard indicates. Not for long, however.

Toss. Crunch. Ace.

"Game to Laver. The games stand five-all, fifth set."

A deuce set now, sudden death, one error can end it.

"Remember when you're out there on the court against the Aussies, Bill . . ."—the voice comes floating back to me from a distance of more than twenty years—". . . you aren't playing only for yourself. You're here at Forest Hills as a Davis Cup player. Today you're representing your country. You won't hear the umpire say, 'Advantage, Talbert.' He'll say, 'Advantage, the United States.' Keep that in mind and live up to it."

I look across the net and see another Australian.

Toss. Crunch. *My* ace. Hooray!

"Fifteen-love," the umpire says.

Laver looks surprised but completely unruffled. My next two serves come back as fast as bullets.

"Fifteen-thirty," the umpire says.

Now I'm in trouble. He's going for the break. *Boy*, these Australians are tough down the stretch. How many years have they been giving me fits? Like that time down in Melbourne when the Challenge Round was played there. Seixas and Trabert were on the squad, and Ham Richardson, and . . . Wait a minute. Something's coming back.

Two images are merging into focus in my mind—two tennis players, serving in slow motion. One is Ham Richardson, a couple decades ago. The other is Rod Laver, a couple hours ago. Both of them are serving fresh balls.

That's *right!* It was back in the third set. I remember now. Laver was serving with a fresh batch of balls, and he hit every serve to my forehand. The same pattern Richardson fell into in Australia. It's possible that Laver did it knowingly, of course. On the other hand, maybe not. Richardson wouldn't believe us when we spotted it and told him. He acquired the habit wholly unawares.

In the next game, Laver will be serving fresh balls. Come on, Talbert. Just a little longer.

Still adhering pretty closely to my original plan, I serve directly at Laver in the ad court. He knocks the return out of court.

"Thirty-all," the umpire says.

Then I give him a sequence of drop shots and lobs and, retreating under the ball, he slips again.

"Forty-thirty," the umpire says.

Laver's getting angry now and more impatient by the second. I visualize him counting all those dollars in his mind. I tease him with a lazy slice service to the ad court, hoping he'll misplay it out of eagerness. He lashes at it viciously and the ball cracks the tape. It rolls over the top and falls softly.

Damn!

"Deuce," the umpire says.

Look at that little kangaroo grinning over there. He couldn't have picked some *other* time to get that netcord back. No, he had to wait until *now*. This guy is just too much. There's no beating him. He has every shot mastered, he has power to burn, he has lightning-quick reactions, he has a wrist made of steel, he keeps coming at you flat-out from morning till night, and as if that weren't enough, the guy gets *lucky*. Why do they even make him show up for the tournament? Why not just *mail* him the trophy?

"You can't play good tennis when you're all hot and bothered, boy. Stall any time you get upset." More advice from my public courts instructor in Cincinnati. "Take a deep breath. Get hold of yourself. Don't be in any great hurry to serve. Look around the galleries. You might have some fans there."

I glance across the side lines and see my father, long dead now, peeking from behind a tree. That's where he stood to watch me play as a kid, so his parental partiality wouldn't embarrass me. He's too far away for me to hear what he's saying, but he's shaking a clenched fist in encouragement.

Calmer now, determined not to give the match away at least, I serve another wide slice to the deuce court. Laver goes for broke with his backhand return. I race after it but slip on the grass and fall down. The ball drops six inches behind the base line.

"Advantage, Talbert."

Rod allows my next serve to go by him untouched, under the impression that I've delivered a fault, too wide. The linesman's call holds, and I've slipped away again.

"Game to Talbert," the umpire says. "Talbert leads, six games to five, fifth set."

Everything rides on this next one now. Laver will be serving with a fresh batch of balls and I'm keeping my fingers crossed. Normally, fresh balls are to the server's advantage. They're hard to return because the fuzz is tight; they sail. But I'm hoping I've detected a pattern in Rod's play that will allow me to

anticipate his serve and get a jump on it. A pattern will sometimes creep into even the best player's game, and if you spot
it, you can use it to defeat him. One time in a Challenge Round
match in Australia, when I was down there as the captain of
the American Davis Cup team, Tony Trabert was playing Lew
Hoad. From the side lines, I picked up a pattern in Hoad's play.
On his backhand side, when the ball came to him high, he
would always hit his return shot down the line. When it came
to him low, he drove it cross-court with spin. I alerted Trabert
to it during the next change of sides, and from then on, being
able to anticipate Lew's backhands, Tony was in control of the
match.

My plan now is to anticipate a serve to my forehand. Usually,
Laver mixes up his services beautifully; by the time you can
tell where one is coming, it's gone. His concealment of *all* his
shots, in fact, is perfect. It's one of his biggest assets. But the
last game he served with a fresh batch of tennis balls, he hit
every serve to my forehand. I'm banking on his doing it again.

Laver seemed a bit put out with himself for letting me off
the hook that time, but I imagine he feels complacent about
this one—his serve, and fresh balls in the bargain. Don't tip your
hand, Talbert. Don't get overeager. If he senses you leaning,
he'll switch and hit behind you. But the *instant* he's committed,
get moving.

Toss. Crunch. I meet the ball exactly where I'd hoped to,
and stroke it down the line past Laver's forehand.

"Love-fifteen," says the umpire.

Rod appears surprised again, but not especially worried. He
probably thinks the shot was just a fluke. Good.

Toss. Crunch. I meet it at the same spot again. Again I
return it with moderate pace, just beyond the reach of Laver's
outstretched forehand, being careful not to get it too close to
the side lines. I don't intend to blow my last chance with

grandstand plays. On a wet court, I can keep the ball farther in bounds without Laver being able to get to it.

"Love-thirty," the umpire says.

Now he has to do a little thinking over there. He kneels down as if to tie his shoes, but he's just stalling. He has to be wondering if he's tipping me off somehow—perhaps by glancing briefly at the spot he's going to serve to; maybe by the way he tosses the ball up; or possibly it's something in his stance or how his feet are placed. Please, Lord, don't let him catch on.

Toss. Crunch. It's right there where I want it again. This time he reaches my return but hits it out.

"Love-forty," the umpire says.

Now I hear another voice, a younger voice, a child. "Were you really that good, Dad?" it's saying. My two boys are sprawled on the living room carpet leafing through some of my scrap-books. They never saw me play when I was up there at the top, and I think they have some doubts that the figure in those clip-pings is the same man they see seated across the room. "Were you really one of the best tennis players in the world? How would you have done against Laver?"

Toss. Crunch. It's coming to my forehand again. I attack it as if this were 1944, as if time had stood still at Forest Hills, and I rip it down the line with all my strength. Laver lunges desperately, but it's past before he gets there. It's a duster. Chalk rises from the base line.

"Game, set, and match scores Talbert," says the umpire.

I think I'll just sit here on the side lines awhile and try to get some of my breath back. I'm all tuckered out from giving Laver such a thrashing. And I want to hear the echo of that announcement again. Those must be the most beautiful words in the language: "Game, set, and match to Talbert."

But all dreams end, and I must float back to earth now and re-enter the harsher world of reality. Unfortunately for those of us who wanted an American to win, what really happened in the semifinals that gloomy afternoon was that Laver defeated Ashe in straight sets, 8–6, 6–3, 14–12. Only in my imaginary match played in jest did the Rocket succumb to a Yank. In the finals, Rod's opponent was Tony Roche, another Aussie— a battle between two left-handers. The pattern of the match was one Laver often follows. After Roche took the first set, nine games to seven, Laver swept the next three with relative ease—the scores were 6–1, 6–2, 6–2—to wrap up not only the United States championship but an unprecedented second Grand Slam. He's quite a tennis player, Mr. Laver is.

You could be too, if you've read this book thoroughly and if you follow the suggestions I've offered along the way. I've let you in on most of what I know about tennis—from how to hold the racket in a proper eastern grip to how to beat a superior player. All you have to do now is to put it into practice. As the saying goes, the ball's in your court.

GLOSSARY OF TENNIS TERMS

ACE. A serve the receiver is unable to get his racket on—the equivalent of a strikeout pitch in baseball. The word is also used as a verb. The server aces his opponent.

AD. A common abbreviation of the word "advantage," used in keeping score after a game reaches deuce. If Laver wins the next point after deuce, for example, the score is given as "Advantage Laver" or, less formally, "Laver's ad."

AD COURT. Another name for the left service court, to which the serve is delivered when the score is someone's ad. "Ad court" is a better designation than "backhand court" because many tennis players are left-handed.

AD-IN. A scorekeeping term that omits the server's name but indicates that the score is his ad. If Laver, while serving, wins the next point after deuce, the score is "Advantage Laver" or "ad-in."

AD-OUT. A scoring term that indicates the receiver's advantage; the opposite of ad-in.

ALLEY. The area, four and a half feet wide, added to each side of a singles court to make it a doubles court.

AMERICAN TWIST. A spin serve delivered with a snap of the wrist that causes the ball, after landing in the service court, to kick off sharply to the receiver's left when delivered by a right-handed server.

ANGLE VOLLEY. A stroke hit before the ball touches the ground and angled past an opponent.

APPROACH SHOT. A running-in shot (a synonymous term) behind which a player advances to the net. He hits it deep to give him time to get there.

AUSTRALIAN FORMATION. An alignment used by the serving team in doubles, in which the net man stands on the same side of the court as the server, forcing the return to be made down the line. The server then follows a diagonal path to the net to fill the net man's normal position.

BACKCOURT. The area, eighteen feet deep, between the service line and the base line.

BACKSPIN. A rotary motion applied by undercutting the ball so that it spins in the opposite direction of its flight path. Also called underspin.

BASE LINE. The rear boundry at each end of the court.

"BIG GAME." An aggressive style of play in which a typical point consists of a fierce serve followed to the net, where a hard volley quickly decides it.

BYE. A device used in early rounds of elimination tournaments to bring into the next round a more manageable number of players, generally a power of two (two, four, eight, sixteen, thirty-two, and so on). Players who receive first-round byes qualify automatically for the second round without having to play a match.

CANNONBALL. A flat, powerful serve given maximum speed.

"CATCH HIM LEANING." To hit behind a player who anticipates a shot and starts moving prematurely in what becomes the wrong direction.

CENTER MARK. A mark, four inches long, that shows the mid-point of the base line. The server must stand on the appropriate side of it.

CENTER SERVICE LINE. The boundary that divides the forecourt into right and left service courts. It is also called the half court line.

"CHASES HIS SERVE." Descriptive of a player whose toss is uncontrolled; he must chase the ball with his racket before he can serve it.

CHIP. A synonym for chop.

CHOP. A stroke in which the ball is given underspin or backspin.

CONSOLATION TOURNAMENT. A loser's bracket competition often incorporated in major tournaments so that players eliminated in early rounds have an apportunity to play more tennis.

CONTINENTAL GRIP. A compromise about halfway between the eastern forehand and eastern backhand grips, used by some players to eliminate the necessity of shifting their hand on the racket. It is also known as the service grip because it's the grip most commonly used in serving.

CROSS-COURT SHOT. A ball hit diagonally to the opposite side of the court—as opposed to a shot hit down the line, whose flight path is roughly parallel to the side line.

CROSSOVER. A tactic employed by the serving team in doubles, in which the net man moves across the center in a poach and the server follows a diagonal path to the net to cover the court vacated by his partner. It is also known as a "scissors."

DEFAULT. To lose a match through a failure to show up on time or an inability to continue playing.

DEUCE. An even score after three or more points have been won by each player or team in a game. A score of 40–40 is deuce.

DEUCE COURT. Another name for the right service court, to which the serve is delivered when the score stands at deuce.

DEUCE SET. An even score in games after ten or more are played. A set in which the games stand 5–5 is a deuce set. It's the equivalent of an extra-inning game in baseball since more than the usual six games are needed to win it.

DINK. A general term for any kind of spin shot plopped softly over the net.

DOUBLE FAULT. The failure of the server—which costs him the point—to put either his first or second service into play.

DOWN-THE-LINE. A shot hit roughly parallel to the side line, as distinguised from a cross-court shot.

DRAW. The schedule of matches for an elimination tournament.

DRIFT. A variation of the poach, in which the net man on the serving team in doubles edges toward the center of the court—first slowly, then more quickly—to a position where he can handle a cross-court return.

DRIVE. A shot hit with a full stroke, either forehand or backhand, after the bounce.

DROP SHOT. A soft stroke hit with backspin that lands just beyond the net.

DROP VOLLEY. A drop shot hit off a ball on the fly. Also called a stop volley.

DUMP. A tactic by which one player eases up during a set or part of a set, expecting to lose that set as a consequence, but hoping to save enough energy in the process for an all-out effort in the next set. A synonymous term is "junk." He junks the set.

DUSTER. A slang term for a shot that hits the line and sprays chalk. Such a ball is considered to have landed in bounds.

EASTERN GRIP. The standard "shake hands" tennis grip, which must be rotated for backhand strokes.

ELIMINATION TOURNAMENT. Competition in which the field of players is cut in half every round, one loss dropping a player from contention.

FAULT. The failure of the server to put his first serve in play.

FINALS. The deciding match between the last two undefeated players in an elimination tournament.

"FISH." Slang for an opponent who's an easy mark, a loser. Synonymous with "pigeon" and "rabbit."

FLAT. Descriptive of a serve given very little spin and consequently hard to control.

FOOT FAULT. A fault called on a server for stepping on or over the base line before his racket touches the ball.

FORCING SHOT. Any shot with which one player assumes the initiative, forcing his opponent into an error or weak return or putting him in an awkward position.

FORECOURT. The area, twenty-one feet deep, between the net and the service line.

GAME. The unit of scoring between the point and the set. It takes four points to win a game, six games to win a set—unless either the game or the set reaches deuce, in which case play continues indefinitely until someone gets two points (or two games) ahead.

"GET THE ELBOW." A slang expression meaning to choke up, to get the jitters. Also referred to as "getting the lump" or "getting the steelies."

GRAND SLAM. A feat that consists of winning the four most coveted titles in the world—the Australian, French, English, and United States singles championships—all in a single year. It has been accomplished by only two men in history, Don Budge in 1938 and Rod Laver in 1962 and 1969.

GROUND STROKE. Any shot hit after it has bounced, as opposed to a volley, which is hit on the fly.

HALF COURT LINE. Another name for the center service line, which separates the right and left service courts.

HALF VOLLEY. A misleading name for a pick-up shot, a ball hit immediately after it bounces—misleading because a volley, by definition, is a ball hit on the fly.

HOLD SERVE. For a player to win the games in which he serves.

"JERK HIM AROUND." To get the better of an opponent, especially by overpowering him; to tie him up in knots.

JUNK. An inclusive slang term for all soft, off-speed shots. Also used in another sense as a synonym for "dump."

"KEEPING HIM HONEST." Hitting to the spot just vacated by a poaching net man in order to discourage him from poaching.

LADDER. A challenge system of competition in which any number of players are listed on a chart set up like the rungs of a ladder. Each player can challenge either of the next two above him, and if the challenger wins, they change positions. Some ladders are maintained for as long as a year, with the champion the player who ends up on top.

LET. Any stroke that for some reason is replayed without penalty. The most common type of let is a serve that ticks the net but lands in the proper court. Sometimes this is mistakenly referred to as a "net" serve; the accurate term is "let."

LINESMAN. An official whose main duty is to determine whether the ball lands within the proper area of the court. In major tournaments, a separate linesman is assigned to each boundary.

LOB. Any ball lofted high in the air, usually over the head of an opponent. Offensive lobs are meant to win points outright by surprising an opponent too close to the net. Defensive lobs, which are usually hit much higher, are intended to allow enough time to recover from a vulnerable position. In England and Australia, the lob is called a "toss."

LOVE. A scoring term synonymous with "zero" or "nothing."

"LOVE, LOVE." Scorekeeping shorthand that designates a shutout, a best-of-three match in which the sets were 6–0, 6–0. On occasions when the winner's score is the usual six games, only the loser's score is unknown. Thus the winner of a match that went 6–2, 6–1 is said to have won it "two, one."

MATCH. A competition between two players or teams that consists of a predetermined number of sets or games.

MATCH POINT. The last point needed to win a match. Double match point is when the player ahead in the match leads 40–15 or 15–40 in match game; in other words, if he wins either of the next two points, he wins the match. Triple match point is when he leads 40–0 or 0–40; any of the next three points would give him the match.

"MUG HUNTER." A player inordinately fond of winning trophies. The term has an unflattering connotation among top players, since mug hunters prefer tournaments where they'd rank among the favorites to those that hold the challenge of stiffer competition, which would diminish their chances of taking home the hardware.

NET BALL. Any shot after the serve that touches the net but remains in play.

NET GAME. A style of play that depends largely on overheads and volleys hit from a position near the net.

NETCORD. A shot hit into the tape at the top of the net which rolls over and falls on the opposite side, thereby deciding the point.

NO MAN'S LAND. The area between the base line and the service line, where lingering is ill-advised.

ON SERVE. Said of a match in progress that has not had a service break; each player has won the games he has served.

ONE-UP-AND-ONE-BACK. A tandem formation used in playing doubles, now generally considered outdated.

OVERHEAD. A ball smashed from a high position off a lob.

OVERSPIN. A rotary motion that accentuates the forward movement of the ball, as if it were turning somersaults. Synonymous with top-spin.

PACE. A desirable combination of speed and "stuff." A fast shot with "something on it" is said to carry pace.

PASSING SHOT. A ball that an opponent playing near the net is unable to get his racket on.

PLACEMENT. Any shot hit out of an opponent's reach.

POACH. The invasion by one member of a doubles team of his partner's normal territory.

"PUT AWAY." To hit a shot so well that no return can be made.

QUARTER FINALS. The round in an elimination tournament in which the field is reduced from eight players to four.

RALLY. A relatively long exchange of shots before a point is finally decided.

"READ." To anticipate accurately an opponent's moves, usually with the help of small clues. A player who is reading his adversary well enjoys a decided advantage.

RECEIVER. The player who receives the serve.

REFEREE. The off-court official in charge of a tournament, as opposed to the umpire, the on-court official in charge of a particular match.

RETRIEVER. A player who excels at running down and returning hard shots.

REVERSE BACKHAND. A shot hit backwards over the net by a player facing the other direction.

REVERSE FORMATION. Another term for the Australian or tandem formation.

ROUND ROBIN. A tournament in which each entrant plays every other entrant an equal number of times. The winner is the one with the best won-and-lost record.

ROUND OF SIXTEEN. The round in an elimination tournament in which the field is reduced from sixteen players to eight.

SCISSORS. Another name for the crossover tactic used in doubles; a delayed Australian formation.

SEEDING. The process by which top-rated players in elimination tournaments are deliberately separated from each other in the draw so they won't meet in early rounds—the aim being to delay a confrontation of the favorites until the later stages of the tournament.

SEMIFINALS. The round in an elimination tournament in which the field is reduced from four players to two.

SERVE. (Also service; the terms are synonymous.) The act of putting the ball into play.

SERVER. The player who puts the ball into play.

SERVICE BREAK. A game in which the server or the serving team loses.

SERVICE COURT. The area in which the serve must land for the ball to be in play. Each service court, left and right, is twenty-one feet deep and thirteen and a half feet wide. The service courts for doubles are the same as for singles.

SERVICE LINE. The back boundary of the service courts, twenty-one feet from the net.

SET. The unit of scoring between the game and the match. Six games win a set unless the games stand five-all, in which case play continues until someone gets two ahead.

SET POINT. The last point needed to win a set. Double set point is when the player ahead in the set leads 40–15 or 15–40 in set game; if he wins either of the next two points, he wins the set. Triple set point is when he leads 40–0 or 0–40; any of the next three points would give him the set.

SIDE-BY-SIDE FORMATION. The normal alignment after the service in doubles, as contrasted to the outdated one-up-and-one-back system.

SIDE SERVICE LINE. The outside boundary of the service court. In singles, the side service line is also the side line.

SIDE LINES. The left and right boundaries of the playing surface.

SITTER. Any shot that hangs invitingly in the air, easy to return for a winner.

SLICE. A stroke to which heavy sidespin is imparted. It breaks to a right-handed player's left as he delivers it.

SMASH. An overhead stroke hit forcefully, intended to win the point outright.

SPIN. The rotating motion of the ball in any direction.

STOP VOLLEY. A drop shot hit on the fly; a drop volley.

"SWEET SPOT." The area in the center of the racket head—ideally, the section of the strings that strikes the ball. A stroke launched from the sweet spot carries maximum pace and is easier to control than one hit near the rim.

TANDEM FORMATION. Another name for the Australian or reverse formation, in which the net man on a doubles team, when his partner is serving, stands on the same side of the court.

THREE-BOUNCE RULE. A modification of the official rules that encourages longer rallies. It prohibits both players from advancing to the net until the ball has bounced three times.

TIE. A series of matches between two tennis teams, as in Davis Cup competition. The United States won its tie with Romania in 1969 by the score of five matches to love.

TOPSPIN. A rotary motion imparted to the ball by stroking up and over it. The same thing as overspin.

TOSS. In America, the act of throwing the ball up before serving it.

In England and Australia, a high-lofted shot—what Americans call a lob.

TWIST. A serve hit with a combination of topspin and sidespin, which gives the ball a kicking action off the ground.

UMPIRE. The ranking official for a particular match. He can overrule a call by a linesman.

UNDERSPIN. A rotary motion applied to the ball in opposition to its flight path. A synonym for backspin.

USLTA. The United States Lawn Tennis Association. The governing organization for amateur tennis in America.

VASSS. Van Alen Simplified Scoring System, similar to the scoring used in table tennis.

VOLLEY. Any stroke hit on the fly, before it bounces.

WESTERN GRIP. An outmoded manner of holding the racket, awkward for returning low shots.

"WRONG FOOT." To hit behind an opponent who starts moving the other way. To "wrong foot" an opponent is the same as to "catch him leaning."